Lone Pine Publishing

Annuals *for* Minnesota *and* Wisconsin

Don Engebretson
Don Williamson

First printed in 2004 10 9 8 7 6 5 4 3 2 1
Printed in Canada

Distributed by: Lone Pine Publishing
1808 – B Street NW, Suite 140
Auburn, WA, USA 98001
Website: www.lonepinepublishing.com

National Library of Canada Cataloguing in Publication Data

Engebretson, Don, 1955–
Annuals for Minnesota and Wisconsin / Don Engebretson, Don Williamson.

Includes index.
ISBN 1-55105-381-0

1. Annuals (Plants)—Minnesota. 2. Annuals (Plants)—Wisconsin.
I. Williamson, Don, 1962– II. Title.
SB422.E54 2004 635.9'312'09776 C2003-907158-8

Editorial Director: Nancy Foulds
Project Editor: Sandra Bit
Editorial: Shelagh Kubish, Lee Craig
Illustrations Coordinator: Carol Woo
Photo Editor: Don Williamson
Research: Alison Beck, Laura Peters
Production Manager: Gene Longson
Book Design: Heather Markham
Layout & Production: Heather Markham, Elliot Engley, Ian Dawe, Chia-Jung Chang
Cover Design: Gerry Dotto
Scanning & Digital Film: Elite Lithographers Co.

Photography: all photos by Tim Matheson or Tamara Eder except
AAS Selection 77a, 101a, 125b, 189a, 221a, 222a, 223a&b, 274b; Linda Oyama Bryan 95a, 97b; David Cavagnaro 228; Elliot Engley 26a, 29, 30a,b&c, 31a&b; EuroAmerican 107a, 126, 127b, 128a&b, 129a, 149b, 200b; Derek Fell 35, 71a, 72b, 123a, 124b, 203a, 212, 213a&b, 214a&b, 215b, 229a&b; Joan de Grey 211b, 215a; Anne Gordon 210, 267b; Saxon Holt 57a; Debra Knapke 57b, 58, 59b, 157b, 158a; Janet Loughrey 209b; Kim O'Leary 26c, 46, 47, 59a, 73a, 111a, 119a&b, 120b, 123b, 125a, 129b, 131a, 155b, 161a&b, 174, 175a&b, 193a, 195b, 243a, 270b; Allison Penko 71b, 211a; Robert Ritchie 43, 45; Aleksandra Szywala 72a, 202; 203b; Peter Thompstone 19a, 53b, 55b, 63b, 73b, 114, 115a, 158c, 171a&b, 172b; Don Williamson 74b, 105b, 138, 139, 207a.

Cover photos: by Tim Matheson except where noted. *Clockwise from top left:* fuchsia, sunflower, dahlia, gazania, sweet potato vine (Tamara Eder), zinnia (Tamara Eder), Mexican sunflower (Tamara Eder), gazania.

Frost date charts: data from the Midwestern Climate Center, Champaign, IL and the Minnesota Department of Natural Resources (www.dnr.state.mn.us/faq/mnfacts/climate.html).

We acknowledge the financial support of the Government of Canada through the Book Publishing Industry Development Program (BPIDP) for our publishing activities.

PC: P1

Contents

Acknowledgments

We gratefully acknowledge all who were involved in this project, as well as the many gorgeous public and private gardens that provided the setting for photographs in this book. Special thanks are extended to the following individuals and organizations: Barbara and Douglas Bloom, Thea and Don Bloomquist, Heidi Clausen, Robert Ritchie, Peter Thompstone, Calvin Glenn of the Minnesota Dahlia Society, Agriculture Canada Central Experimental Farm, Bordine Nursery, Casa Loma Gardens, Chicago Botanic Gardens, Cranbrook Gardens, Cranbrook Garden Auxiliary, Cullen Gardens, Edwards Gardens, Inniswood Metro Gardens, Montreal Botanic Garden, Morton Arboretum, Niagara Parks Botanical Gardens and Royal Botanical Gardens.

My thanks to all the good people at Lone Pine Publishing and to all the professional growers of the exquisite annuals that have crossed, and on some occasions edged, my path.—*Don Engebretson*

I would like to express my appreciation to all the wonderful people involved in this project. Special thanks are extended to all the photographers that helped fill our book with all the great pictures you see, and to the many sources of information and inspiration that helped fill this book with all the great information you read. I also thank The Creator.—*Don Williamson*

The Flowers at a Glance

A PICTORIAL GUIDE IN ALPHABETICAL ORDER

Cape marigold p. 92

Canterbury bells p. 90

Celosia p. 94

China aster p. 98

Cleome p. 100

Coleus p. 104

Coreopsis p. 108

Cosmos p. 110

Cup flower p. 114

Dahlberg daisy p. 116

Dahlia p. 118

Dianthus p. 122

Dusty miller p. 130

Dwarf morning glory p. 132

Diascia p. 126

English daisy p. 134

Felicia p. 136

Flowering flax p. 138

Flowering tobacco
p. 140

Forget-me-not
p. 144

Four o'clocks
p. 146

Fuchsia
p. 148

Gaura
p. 152

Gazania
p. 154

Geranium
p. 156

Heliotrope
p. 164

Globe amaranth
p. 160

Godetia
p. 162

Hollyhock
p. 168

Impatiens
p. 170

Larkspur
p. 176

Lantana
p. 174

Lavatera
p. 178

Lisianthus
p. 182

Love-in-a-mist
p. 186

Madagascar periwinkle
p. 188

Lobelia
p. 184

Marigold
p. 190

Mexican sunflower
p. 194

Monkey flower
p. 196

Morning glory
p. 198

Ornamental kale
p. 210

Musk mallow
p. 202

Nasturtium
p. 204

Nemesia
p. 208

Osteospermum
p. 212

Pentas
p. 218

Petunia
p. 220

Pimpernel
p. 224

Painted-tongue
p. 216

Pincushion flower
p. 226

Polka dot plant
p. 228

Poor man's orchid
p. 230

Portulaca p. 238

Salvia p. 240

Poppy p. 234

Snapdragon p. 244

Statice p. 248

Stock p. 250

Summer forget-me-not p. 252

Sweet pea p. 262

Sunflower p. 254

Swan River daisy p. 258

Sweet alyssum p. 260

Transvaal daisy p. 264

Violet p. 272

Verbena p. 268

Wishbone flower p. 276

Zinnia p. 278

INTRODUCTION

REGARDLESS OF YOUR GARDEN'S SIZE, SHAPE OR STYLE, THE ADDITION of blooming annuals is key to creating an attractive, unique and colorful floral landscape. Annuals are popular because they produce abundant flowers in a wide variety of colors over a long period of time. Many annuals are adapted to a variety of growing conditions, from hot, dry sun to cool, damp shade.

Annuals are easy and fun to grow. As you explore the seemingly endless varieties that flourish in our northern region, and gain confidence in their use, your natural design style will quickly evolve. Some gardeners discover they prefer annuals as subtle accents, tucking single plants or small groupings into the perennial/shrub garden to add a dash of color or texture. Unabashed color worshippers discover that entire beds of annuals best express their concept of what a garden should be.

True annuals are plants that complete their full life cycle—they germinate, mature, bloom, set seed and die—in one growing season. Some plants grown as annuals are actually biennials, tender perennials or even shrubs; these plants cannot survive our winters but grow quickly enough to be planted anew each year. Each plant described in this book falls into one of these categories.

Annuals make great plant choices for Minnesota and Wisconsin because most are adaptable to our variable summers. Given enough moisture, they can generally handle 90° F or a sudden cool snap. Much of our region receives 20–30" of precipitation per year, with slightly more rain in Wisconsin than in Minnesota. This is generally enough moisture to support a wide range of plants, though even if you assign an inch of water per week as the optimal amount, you will still need to provide some supplemental moisture.

The length of the growing season and geographic latitude determine how long annuals last in the garden. In Wisconsin and Minnesota, the last killing frost can occur at any time between April 1 and May 31 (see charts on page 13). Lake Michigan and Lake Superior, as well as other large lakes, moderate late cold snaps and early fall chills, extending the growing season a couple of weeks in areas near them. In some northern Minnesota counties, there may be fewer than 150 frost-free days each year versus more than 190 in the south of Wisconsin. All Minnesota and Wisconsin gardeners can expect a frost-free period of between four to six months, plenty of time for annuals to mature and fill the garden with color.

Soil temperature is a factor in determining when to plant in spring. Many annual seeds need warm soil to germinate, and some plants may grow slowly if planted into cool soil. The plant entries in this book indicate minimum soil temperatures for seeding or planting out. Use an inexpensive soil thermometer, available at most garden centers, to help you determine the right time to seed different plants. For gardeners who like to plant before the last spring frost, this book will help you determine which annuals are worth the early gamble and which require more patience.

The selection of annuals increases every year. There are always newly developed cultivars to try, often with an expanded color range or increased disease resistance. Some beautiful plants that have been overlooked in the past because they bloom later in summer are now in wider use. New species have been introduced from other parts of the world. The use of heritage varieties has been revived because many gardeners are concerned with overhybridization or appreciate that many older varieties have more fragrance.

When some new varieties are introduced, they may experience a short period of popularity but are soon forgotten. Others are entered in trials that compare each variety to a similar one already on the market. These trials are conducted across the United States and Canada. The varieties judged superior in many regions are certified as All-America Selections. These varieties should perform well in most gardens. Look for the distinctive 'All-America Selections Winner' symbol in seed catalogs and on plant tags at garden centers and nurseries, or visit the AAS website.

Dusty miller, shown with marigold and canna lily, is grown for its silvery foliage.

AVERAGE LAST SPRING FROST DATES

Minnesota

LOCATION	MONTH
ALBERT LEA	2-MAY
ALEXANDRIA	8-MAY
BAUDETTE	22-MAY
BEMIDJI	22-MAY
BRAINERD	12-MAY
CAMBRIDGE	8-MAY
CROOKSTON	16-MAY
DULUTH AIRPORT	20-MAY
DULUTH HARBOUR	29-APR
FAIRMONT	1-MAY
FARIBAULT	10-MAY
FERGUS FALLS	9-MAY
GRAND MARAIS	15-MAY
GRAND RAPIDS	23-MAY
HALLOCK	19-MAY
LONG PRAIRIE	16-MAY
LUVERNE	7-MAY
MADISON	7-MAY
MEADOWLANDS	3-JUN
MINNEAPOLIS/ST. PAUL	29-APR
MOORHEAD	13-MAY
NORTH MANKATO	4-MAY
PIPESTONE	12-MAY
ROCHESTER	8-MAY
ST. CLOUD	12-MAY
WHEATON	10-MAY
WILLMAR	2-MAY
WINDOM	7-MAY
WINONA	27-APR

Wisconsin

LOCATION	MONTH
APPLETON	2-MAY
ASHLAND	3-JUN
BELOIT	27-APR
BLAIR	18-MAY
CRIVITZ	26-MAY
EAU CLAIRE	10-MAY
GREEN BAY	10-MAY
KENOSHA	30-APR
LA CROSSE	30-APR
MADISON	12-MAY
MANITOWOC	9-MAY
MILWAUKEE	29-APR
MINOCQUA	28-MAY
OCONTO	13-MAY
OSHKOSH	9-MAY
PARK FALLS	16-MAY
PLATTEVILLE	9-MAY
PORTAGE	14-MAY
PRAIRIE DU CHIEN	4-MAY
RACINE	2-MAY
RHINELANDER	20-MAY
RICHLAND CENTER	11-MAY
RIVER FALLS	8-MAY
SPOONER	27-MAY
ST. CROIX FALLS	11-MAY
STEVENS POINT	9-MAY
SUPERIOR	12-MAY
WAUSAU	8-MAY
WISCONSIN DELLS	11-MAY

Annual Gardens

ANNUALS ARE SHORT-LIVED, ALLOWING GARDENERS FLEXIBILITY and freedom when planning their gardens. While trees and shrubs form the permanent structure or the 'bones' of the garden, and perennials and groundcovers occupy the spaces between them, annuals add bold patterns and bright splashes of color. Include annuals anywhere that you would like an extra splash of color—in pots staggered up porch steps or on a deck, in windowsill planters or in hanging baskets. Even well-established gardens are brightened by the addition of annual flowers.

Annuals are perfect for filling in bare spaces around small or leggy shrubs or between perennials that bloom late in the season. Annual vines can create a temporary screen to hide an undesirable view or an unattractive part of the garden. When planning your garden, consult as many sources as you can for advice, and make a list of the plants you would like to include in your garden.

Finding the right annuals for your garden will require experimentation, creativity and planning. Most people make the color, size and shape of the blossoms their prime considerations. Other attributes to consider are the size and shape of the whole plant and its leaves. Including a variety of flowers and plant sizes, shapes and colors will make your garden more interesting. Consult the Quick Reference Chart on pp. 282–87 to help you plan.

Annuals of different colors affect us differently. The cool colors—purple, blue and green—are soothing and relaxing, so annuals such as lobelia, ageratum and browallia can make a small garden appear larger. The warm colors—red, orange and yellow—are more stimulating, so annuals such as scarlet salvia, calendula and Mexican sunflower appear to fill larger spaces. Warm colors can make even the

Ageratum provides cool color.

Calendula provides warm color.

largest, most imposing garden welcoming.

If you have time to enjoy your garden only in the evenings, consider pale colors. White and yellow show up well at dusk and even at night. Some plants have flowers that open only in the evenings, often with a fragrance that further enhances the evening garden. Moonflower (*Ipomoea alba*) is a twining plant with large, white, fragrant flowers that open when the sun sets.

Some annuals are grown solely for their appealing or colorful foliage and can look particularly attractive in mixed hanging baskets and planters. Some foliage plants, such as coleus, are so striking that they can be used on their own as specimens; others, such as dusty miller, provide an interesting contrast to brightly colored flowers. Use annuals creatively to produce eye-catching contrasts with the plants nearby.

Annuals with Interesting Foliage

- Amaranth 'Illumination'
- Coleus
- Dusty Miller
- Geranium
- Nasturtium
- Polka dot plant
- Rex begonia
- Sweet potato vine

Texture is another element to consider when planning a garden. Both flowers and foliage have a visual texture. Large leaves appear coarse, making a garden seem smaller and more shaded. Coarse-textured flowers look bold and dramatic and can be seen from a distance. Small leaves appear fine, creating a sense of increased space and light. Fine-textured flowers look soothing and even a bit mysterious. Some annuals have flowers and foliage with contrasting textures. Using a variety of textures helps make a garden captivating and appealing.

Coarse-textured Annuals

- Amaranth
- Angel's trumpet
- Flowering tobacco
- Hollyhock
- Opium poppy
- Sunflower
- Sweet potato vine
- Zinnia

Fine-textured Annuals

- Baby's breath
- Cup flower
- Gaura
- Larkspur
- Lobelia
- Love-in-a-mist
- Swan River daisy
- Sweet alyssum

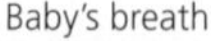

Sweet potato vine

Baby's breath

Opium poppy

GETTING STARTED

BEFORE BUYING OR PLANTING YOUR ANNUALS, CONSIDER THE growing conditions in your garden. These conditions will influence not only the types of plants that you select, but also the locations in which you plant them. For hot, dry areas or for low-lying, damp sections, select plants that prefer those conditions. The plants will be healthier and less susceptible to problems if grown in optimum conditions. Match the plants to the garden not the garden to the plants.

Light levels, soil texture, pH, fertility, the amount of exposure in your garden and the plants' frost tolerance provide guidelines for selecting your plants. Sketching your garden may help you visualize the various conditions. Your sketch should include shaded areas, low-lying or wet areas and exposed or windy sections. Consult the Quick Reference Chart on pp. 282–87 and the individual plant entries to find annuals suited to those conditions. Experimenting with annuals will, in turn, help you learn about the conditions of your garden.

Light

Four levels of light may be present in a garden: full sun, partial shade (partial sun), light shade and full shade. Available light is affected by buildings, trees, fences and the position of the sun at different times of the day and year. Knowing what light is available in your garden will help you determine what plants to buy and where to place them.

Full sun locations, such as south-facing gardens, receive direct sun for at least six hours a day. Locations classified as partial shade (partial sun), such

Geranium

as east- or west-facing gardens, receive direct morning or late-afternoon sun and then shade for the rest of the day. Light shade locations receive shade for most or all of the day, but some sunlight does filter through to ground level. An example of a light-shade location is the ground under a small-leaved tree such as a birch. Full shade locations, such as under a dense tree canopy, receive no direct sunlight.

Sun-loving plants may become tall and straggly and flower poorly in too much shade. Shade-loving plants may get scorched leaves or even wilt and die if they get too much sun. Many plants tolerate a range of light conditions.

Annuals for Full Sun

Ageratum
Amaranth
Black-eyed Susan
Cleome
Cosmos
Geranium
Marigold
Portulaca
Statice

Annuals for Partial Shade

Baby blue-eyes
Begonia
Browallia
Canterbury bells
Coleus
Impatiens
Violet

Annuals for Sun or Shade

Black-eyed Susan
Black-eyed Susan vine
Cup flower
Flowering tobacco
Lobelia
Morning glory
Snapdragon
Stock

Black-eyed Susan

Soil

Soil quality is an extremely important element of a healthy garden. Plant roots rely on the air, water and nutrients that are held within soil. Plants also depend on soil to hold them upright. In turn, the soil benefits from plant roots breaking down large soil clods. Plants prevent soil erosion by binding together small particles and reducing the amount of exposed surface. When plants die and break down, they add organic nutrients to the soil and feed beneficial microorganisms.

Soil is made up of particles of different sizes. Sand particles are the largest—water drains quickly from sandy soil and nutrients tend to get washed away. Sandy soil does not compact very easily. Clay particles, which are the smallest, can be seen only through a microscope. Clay holds the most nutrients, but it also compacts easily and has little air space. Clay is slow to absorb water and equally slow to let it drain. Silt particles are smaller than sand particles but larger than clay particles. Most soils are loams, composed of a combination of different particle sizes.

The pH level of soil—the indicator of its acidity or alkalinity—influences the availability of nutrients. Most plants thrive in soil with a pH between 6.0 and 7.0. Each garden is different and should be tested, not only for pH but also for nutrient levels. Simple test kits can be purchased at most garden centers. Soil-testing labs in the agriculture departments of both the University of Minnesota and University of Wisconsin can fully analyze soil pH and the levels of various nutrients in your soil and provide comprehensive feedback.

Fan flower with New Guinea impatiens

The addition of elemental sulfur, peat moss or chopped oak leaves will lower soil pH, but it can take several years or more for the effects to become permanent. Acidity can be corrected by adding wood ash, which is extremely alkaline, or horticultural lime. Do not use wood ash from such sources as treated lumber or pallets.

Busy Lizzie impatiens

Wishbone flower

Grow plants that prefer a pH different from that in your garden soil in planters or raised beds, where it is easier to control and alter the soil's pH. Always ask about the pH and other soil properties before you import any soil, purchased or otherwise, into your garden.

California poppy

Water drainage is affected by soil type and terrain in your garden. Plants that prefer well-drained soil and do not require a large amount of moisture grow well on a sloping hillside with rocky soil. Improve water retention in these areas by adding organic matter. Plants that thrive on a consistent water supply or boggy conditions are ideal for low-lying areas that retain water for longer periods or hardly drain at all, such as at the base of a slope. In extremely wet areas, improve drainage by adding pea gravel, installing drainage tile or by building raised beds.

Annuals for Moist Soil

- Ageratum
- Angel's trumpet
- Black-eyed Susan vine
- Cleome
- Impatiens
- Monkey flower
- Violet
- Wishbone flower

Annuals for Dry Soil

- Baby's breath
- Bachelor's buttons
- California poppy
- Coreopsis
- Cosmos
- Marigold
- Mexican sunflower
- Portulaca
- Zinnia

Exposure

Your garden is exposed to wind, heat, cold and rain, and some plants are better adapted than others to withstand the potential damage of these forces. Buildings, walls, fences, hills, hedges, trees and even tall perennials influence and often reduce exposure.

Annuals are often damaged by wind and heat. The sun can be very intense, and heat can rise quickly on a sunny afternoon. Plant annuals that tolerate or even thrive in hot weather in the hot spots in your garden.

Hanging, moss-lined baskets are especially susceptible to wind and heat. Water can evaporate very quickly from all sides of a moss basket, especially in hot or windy locations. Watch for wilting, and water regularly. These baskets will hold up better in adverse conditions if you soak the moss or other liner in a wetting agent, such as Water-In™, which helps water penetrate into dry soils. Add some of the wetting agent to the water when first watering.

Too much rain or overwatering can also damage annuals. Early in the season, seeds or seedlings can be washed away in heavy rain. A light mulch or grow-cover will help prevent this problem. Grow-covers are temporary 'mini-greenhouses,' usually consisting of a series of wire hoops placed along a row of seeds or seedlings, covered with a light, white fabric that allows sun, air and moisture in and keeps bugs, birds and heavy weather out. Established annuals (or their flowers) can be destroyed by heavy rain. Most annuals will recover, but some are slow to do so. For exposed sites, choose plants or varieties that are quick to recover from rain damage.

Frost Tolerance

When planting annuals, consider their ability to tolerate an unexpected frost. Last-frost and first-frost dates vary greatly from year to year and region to region in Wisconsin and Minnesota. They can also vary considerably within each region. The charts on p. 13 give a general idea of when you can expect the last frost in your region; consult your local garden center for more specific information.

Hanging baskets are subject to extreme exposure to the elements.

Annuals are grouped into three categories based on how tolerant they are of cold weather: hardy, half-hardy or tender. The Quick Reference Chart on pp. 282–87 indicates the hardiness of the annuals discussed in this book.

Lavatera is a hardy annual.

Hardy annuals tolerate low temperatures and frost. They can be planted in the garden early and may continue to flower long into fall or even winter. Many hardy annuals are sown directly in the garden before the last-frost date.

Half-hardy annuals can tolerate a light frost but will be killed by a heavy one. These annuals can be planted out around the last-frost date and will generally benefit from being started early from seed indoors.

Tender annuals have no frost tolerance at all and might suffer if the temperatures drop to even just a few degrees above freezing. These plants are often started early indoors and not planted in the garden until the last-frost date has passed and the ground has had a chance to warm up. These annuals often have the advantage of tolerating hot summer temperatures.

Protecting plants from frost is relatively simple. Cover them overnight with sheets, towels, burlap, row covers or even cardboard boxes. Don't use plastic because it doesn't retain heat and won't provide any insulation.

Dahlia (below) and marigold (above) are frost tender.

Preparing the Garden

PROPERLY PREPARING YOUR FLOWERBEDS BEFORE SEEDING OR transplanting saves you time and effort over the summer and prevents many gardening problems. To give your annuals a good start, begin with as few weeds as possible and with a well-prepared soil enriched with organic matter.

Every spring, loosen the soil with a garden fork and remove the weeds. Avoid working the soil when it is very wet or very dry, or you may damage the soil structure by breaking down the pockets that hold air and water. Topdress established beds annually with fresh compost or other types of organic matter, and work fresh organic matter in each spring as you plant. Use a spade or garden fork. Once a bed has become established and contains adequate organic matter, don't till it every year with a power tiller, because this can damage the soil structure.

For containers, use potting mix sold in bags at local nursery centers. Regular garden soil loses its structure in pots, quickly compacting into a solid mass that drains poorly.

Organic matter is a very important component of soil. It increases the water- and nutrient-holding capacity of sandy soil and binds together the large particles. Organic matter increases a clay soil's ability to absorb and drain water by opening up spaces between the tiny particles. Common organic additives for your soil include dried grass clippings, shredded leaves, peat moss, chopped straw, composted rice hulls, well-rotted manure, alfalfa pellets and compost.

Composting

Most organic matter you add to your garden will be of greater benefit if it has been composted first. Composted organic matter adds nutrients and improves soil structure. Decaying organic matter releases acids and helps lower the pH in alkaline soils. If your soil is acidic and has lots of organic matter, amendments and time are needed to raise the pH.

Microorganisms that break down organic matter use the same nutrients as your plants. The fresher and less-decayed the organic matter, the more nutrients in the soil will be used to break it down. As a result, your plants will be robbed of vital nutrients, particularly nitrogen. Also, fresh organic matter and garden debris can encourage or introduce pests and diseases in your garden.

A compost pile or bin creates a controlled environment where organic matter can be fully broken down. Good composting methods also reduce the possibility of spreading pests and diseases. Compost can be made in a pile, in a wooden box or in a purchased compost bin. Two methods can be used; neither is complicated, but the first requires more effort.

Loosen the soil and remove as many weeds and as much debris as possible.

The 'active' or hot composting method requires you to turn the pile every week or so during the growing season. Frequent turning creates compost faster, but because the compost generates a lot of heat, some beneficial microorganisms that help fight diseases may be killed. If you prefer the active approach to composting, check *Perennials for Minnesota and Wisconsin* or any good book on composting.

For many gardeners, 'passive' or cold composting is the more practical approach. Making a passive compost pile involves dumping yard waste into a pile. This material may include weeds pulled from the garden, pruned branches cut into small pieces, leftover grass clippings, fall leaves and fruit and vegetable scraps. Never compost meat scraps. Avoid putting weed seeds and diseased or pest-ridden plants into your compost pile, or you risk spreading problems throughout your garden.

Fallen leaves should be chopped up with a mulching mower before adding them to a compost pile or using them as mulch. Many gardeners collect leaves from neighbors, store them in plastic bags and add them to their compost pile over the following year.

After a season or two, the passive pile will have a layer of pure black gold at the bottom that looks much like the leaf mold found in the woods. Your finished compost can be accessed by moving the top of the pile aside. Spread the finished compost on the surface of the garden bed, or, if compost is in short supply, just add a trowelful to each planting hole.

Many municipalities now recycle yard wastes into compost that is made available to residents. Compost can also be purchased from some garden centers.

Selecting Annuals

MANY GARDENERS CONSIDER THE TRIP TO THE LOCAL GARDEN center to choose their annuals an important rite of spring. Others consider starting their own annuals from seed one of the most rewarding aspects of gardening. Both methods have benefits, and many gardeners use a combination of the two.

Purchasing transplants is usually easier than starting from seed and provides you with plants that are well grown and often already in bloom. Starting seeds can be impractical. It requires space, facilities and time. Some seeds require specific conditions difficult to achieve in a house, or they have erratic germination rates. Other seeds, however, are easy and inexpensive to start. Starting from seed offers you a greater selection because seed catalogs list many more plants than are offered at most garden centers.

Purchased annuals are grown in a variety of containers. Some are sold in individual pots, some in divided cell-packs and others in undivided trays. Each type has its advantages and disadvantages.

Annuals in individual pots are usually well established and have plenty of space for root growth. These annuals were probably seeded in flat trays and then transplanted into individual pots once they developed a few leaves. The cost of labor, pots and soil can make this option somewhat more expensive. If you are planting a large area you may also find it difficult to transport large numbers of plants of this size.

Annuals grown in cell-packs are often inexpensive and hold four to eight plants, making them easy to transport. These annuals suffer less root damage when transplanted than do annuals in undivided trays, but because each cell is quite small, plants may become root-bound quickly.

Healthy seedling removed from cell-pack (above)

Lantana (below) and fuchsia (above) are often available only as transplants.

Annuals grown in undivided trays are also inexpensive. They have plenty of room for root growth and can be left in the trays longer than can plants in other types of containers. Their roots, however, tend to become entangled, making the plants difficult to separate.

Choose plants that are not yet flowering because they are younger and are less likely to be root-bound. Plants covered with flowers have already passed through a significant portion of their rooting stage, and while they will add instant color when planted, they will not perform at their best in the heat of summer. If you buy annuals already in bloom, pinch off the blooms and buds just prior to planting to encourage new root growth and a bigger show of flowers throughout the season.

Check for roots emerging from the holes at the bottom of the cells, or gently remove the plant from the container to look at the roots. An overabundance of roots means that the plant is too mature for the container, especially if the roots are wrapped around the inside of the container in a thick web. Such plants are slow to establish once they are transplanted into the garden.

Plants should be compact and have good color. Healthy leaves look firm and vibrant. Unhealthy leaves may be discolored, chewed or wilted. Tall, leggy plants have likely been deprived of light. Sickly plants may not survive being transplanted and may spread pests or diseases to your garden.

Once you get your annuals home, water them if they are dry. Annuals growing in trays or small containers may require water more than once a day. See p. 27 for information on planting out your new annuals.

Planting Annuals

ONCE YOUR ANNUALS ARE HARDENED OFF, IT IS TIME TO PLANT them out. If you have already prepared your beds (see p. 23), you are ready to start. The only tool you'll likely need is a trowel. Allow enough time to complete the job. Avoid removing plants from their pots and then not planting them. If young plants are left out in the sun, they can quickly dry out and die. It's better to plant in the early morning, in the evening or on an overcast day.

Water plants lightly to help ease them from their containers. Push on the bottom of the cell or pot with your thumb to remove the plants. If the plants were growing in an undivided tray, you will have to gently untangle the roots. Very tangled roots can be separated by immersing them in water and washing off some soil, or by snipping the plants apart with garden scissors. If you must handle the plant, hold it by a leaf to avoid crushing the stems. Remove and discard any damaged growth.

The rootball should contain a network of white roots. If the rootball is densely matted and twisted (rootbound), score the rootball vertically on four sides with a sharp knife or gently break it apart. This encourages new roots, which start from the cuts or breaks, to extend and grow outward.

Insert your trowel into the soil and pull it toward you, creating a wedge.

Annuals planted in drifts (above)

Informal planting (above)
Annual border planted according to height (below)

Place your annual into the hole and firm the soil around the plant with your hands. Water newly planted annuals gently but thoroughly. They need frequent watering for a couple of weeks, until they become established.

Though formal bedding-out patterns are still used in many parks and formal gardens, today's plantings are often made in casual groups and natural drifts. There are more design choices than simple, straight rows. When arranging your garden beds, plant random clusters of three to five annuals to add color and interest. Always plant groups of the same annual in odd numbers for a more natural effect. Space out your annuals by removing them from their containers and randomly placing them on the bed. Prevent the roots from drying out by planting only one small section at a time.

Combine low-growing or spreading annuals with tall or bushy ones. Keep the tallest plants toward the back and smallest plants toward the front of each bed. This arrangement improves the visibility of the plants and hides the often unattractive lower parts of taller plants.

Avoid planting your annuals too far apart. A good rule of thumb is to space 4–6" less than the plant's spread, to create a pleasing, full effect when the plants mature. We suggest spacing distances in each plant entry.

Aside from these general guidelines, there are no strict rules when it comes to planting and spacing. Have fun and create something that you will enjoy for the rest of the season.

Annuals from Seed

STARTING YOUR OWN ANNUALS CAN SAVE YOU MONEY, PARTICULARLY if you have a large area to plant. Germinating seeds in a warm spot, such as on top of the refrigerator, then placing the seedlings on a sunny windowsill is not recommended for northern gardeners. The sun's intensity (particularly when filtered by window glass) is not high enough in late winter and spring to properly grow plants from seed. Plants grown on windowsills usually become thin and leggy and don't perform well when transplanted into the garden.

The preferred method is to start seeds and grow seedlings under artificial light. The basement is a great location to set up a small growing area. You can purchase complete seed-starting growing systems that include adjustable fluorescent lights and growing platforms, or create your own by suspending inexpensive shop lights over a table large enough to hold the number of plants you want to grow. A four-foot square table can be adequately lit by two four-foot shop lights.

Each plant entry in this book will have specific information on starting the annual from seed, but some basic procedures apply to all seeds. Cell-packs in trays with plastic dome covers are useful because the cell-packs keep roots separated, and the tray and dome keep moisture in.

Seeds can also be started in peat pots or peat pellets. The advantage to starting in peat pots or pellets is that you won't disturb the roots when transplanting your annuals. When planting peat pots into the garden, be sure to remove the top couple of inches of pot and then gently slice vertically down each side of the pot. If any of the pot sticks up out of the soil, it can wick moisture away from your plant.

Use a soil mix intended for seedlings. The texture of these mixes is very fine, usually made from peat moss, vermiculite and perlite. The mix will have good water-holding capacity and will have been sterilized to prevent

Preparing seed trays (above)

Use a folded piece of paper to handle tiny seeds.

A mister allows gentle watering (below).

pests and diseases from attacking your tender young seedlings. Using a sterile soil mix, keeping soil evenly moist and maintaining good air circulation will prevent the problem of damping-off. Damping-off is caused by a variety of soil-born fungi, causing the affected seedling to appear to have been pinched at soil level. The pinched area blackens, and the seedling topples over and dies. Damping-off can also be reduced or prevented by spreading a $^1/_4$" layer of peat moss over the seedbed.

Fill your pots, cell-packs or seed trays with the soil mix and firm it down slightly. Soil that is too firmly packed will not drain well. Wetting the soil before planting your seeds helps keep the seeds where you plant them.

Large seeds can be planted one or two to a cell, but smaller seeds may have to be placed in a folded piece of paper and sprinkled evenly over the soil surface. Very tiny seeds, like those of begonias, can be mixed with fine sand before being sprinkled evenly across the soil surface.

Small seeds need not be covered with any more soil, but medium-sized seeds can be lightly covered, and large seeds can be poked into the soil. Seeds of some plants need to be exposed to light in order to germinate. These seeds should be left on the soil surface regardless of their size. Directions on most seed packets will provide this information.

Place pots or flats of seeds in clear plastic bags to retain humidity while the seeds are germinating. Many planting trays come with clear plastic covers, which can be placed over the trays to keep the moisture in. For plants that need heat to germinate, lowering the grow lights to an inch or two above the plastic lid will raise the temperature inside to around 75° F. Remove the plastic once the seeds have germinated. Check the progress of your seedlings daily.

The amount and timing of watering is critical to successfully growing annuals from seed. Most germinated seeds and young seedlings will perish if the soil is allowed to dry out. Strive to maintain a consistently moist soil, which may mean watering lightly every day. As the seedlings get bigger, water less frequently but a little more heavily. Generally, when the seedlings have their first true leaves (those that look like the adult leaves), you can cut back to watering only when the top 1/8" of soil has dried. Once seedlings have emerged, some gardeners set up a small fan to blow air across the table, which reduces the incidence of some fungal diseases and helps the little seedlings grow strong as they bend and sway in the breeze.

Seeds provide all the energy and nutrients that younger seedlings require. Small seedlings do not need to be fertilized until they have about four or five true leaves. Fertilizer will cause the plants to develop soft growth that is more susceptible to insects and diseases, and too strong a fertilizer can burn tender young roots. When the first leaves that sprouted (seed leaves) begin to shrivel, the plant has used up all its seed energy, so you can begin to apply a fertilizer diluted to 1/4 strength.

Seedlings are big enough to transplant when the first true leaves appear. If the seedlings get too big for their containers before you are ready to plant in your garden, you may have to transplant them to larger pots to prevent them from becoming root-bound.

A cover on the seed tray helps keep in moisture.

Harden plants off by exposing them to sunnier, windier conditions and fluctuating outdoor temperatures for increasing periods of time every day for at least a week. Avoid direct sunlight for the first two days. A cold frame is ideal for hardening off plants. It can also be used to protect tender plants over winter, to start seeds early in winter and spring and to start seeds that need a cold treatment. See *Perennials for Minnesota and Wisconsin* for additional information about cold frames.

Annuals with large seeds, quick-germinating seeds or those that are difficult to transplant can be sown

A small table with an adjustable fluorescent light is excellent for starting seeds (below).

Cosmos (above)

Painted-tongue (center)

Pentas (below)

directly in the garden. Start with a well-prepared bed that has been smoothly raked. The small furrows left by the rake will help hold moisture and prevent the seeds from being washed away. Sprinkle the seeds into the furrows and cover them lightly with peat moss or soil. Larger seeds can be planted slightly deeper into the soil. You may not want to sow very tiny seeds directly in the garden because they can blow or wash away.

Keep the soil moist to ensure even germination. Use a gentle spray to avoid washing the seeds around the bed, or they may pool into dense clumps. Cover your newly seeded bed with chicken wire, an old sheet or some thorny branches to discourage pets from digging. A grow-cover also discourages animals and helps speed germination. Remove the cover once the seeds have germinated.

Annuals for Direct Seeding

- Ageratum
- Amaranth
- Baby's breath
- Bachelor's buttons
- Black-eyed Susan
- Calendula
- Canterbury bells
- Cosmos
- Gazania
- Larkspur
- Lavatera
- Nasturtium
- Painted-tongue
- Pentas
- Poppy
- Sunflower
- Sweet pea
- Zinnia

Caring for Annuals

ONGOING MAINTENANCE WILL KEEP YOUR GARDEN LOOKING ITS best. Some annuals require more care than do others, but most require minimal care once established. Weeding, watering, fertilizing, pinching and deadheading are the basic tasks that, when performed regularly, pay dividends throughout the season. As well, some perennials grown as annuals may be overwintered with little effort.

Deadheading dahlias

Weeding

Controlling weed populations keeps the garden healthy and neat. Weeding may not be anyone's favorite task, but it is essential. Weeds compete with your plants for light, nutrients and space and can also harbor pests and diseases.

Pull weeds by hand or with a hoe. It is easiest to pull weeds shortly after a rainfall, when the soil is soft and damp. A hoe scuffed quickly across the soil surface will uproot small weeds and sever larger ones from their roots. Try to pull weeds while they are still small. Once they are large enough to flower, many will quickly set seed. You will then have an entire new generation to worry about.

Mulching

A layer of mulch around your plants will prevent weeds from germinating by preventing sufficient light from reaching their seeds. Those that do germinate will be smothered or will find it difficult to get to the soil surface, exhausting their energy before they get a chance to grow. Weeds are very easy to pull from a mulched bed.

Removing weeds is an important task.

Mulch also helps maintain consistent soil temperatures and allows the soil to better retain moisture, which means you will not need to water as often. In areas that receive heavy wind or rainfall, mulch can protect soil and prevent erosion. Mulching is effective in both garden beds and planters and is especially important where summer temperatures can exceed 90° F.

Organic mulches include compost, finely shredded bark, cocoa bean shells, shredded leaves, dried grass clippings and shredded newsprint (but not glossy paper). These mulches add nutrients to soil as they break down, improving the quality of the soil and ultimately the health of your plants. Shredded cedar bark also contains a naturally occurring fungicide, which can help prevent root rot.

Spread 2–3" of mulch over the soil after you have planted your annuals. As your mulch breaks down over summer, be sure to replenish it. Don't pile mulch too thickly around the crowns and stems of your annuals because doing so traps moisture, prevents air circulation and encourages fungal disease.

Watering

Once your annuals are established, water thoroughly but infrequently, making sure the water penetrates at least 6" into the soil. Annuals given a sprinkle of water every day develop roots that stay close to the soil surface, making the plants vulnerable to heat and dry spells. Annuals given a deep watering once a week develop a deeper root system. In a dry spell they will be adapted to seeking out the water trapped deeper in the ground. Annuals in excessively sunny, hot areas will usually require watering more than once per week.

To prevent water loss to evaporation, apply mulch, and do most of your watering in the morning. This allows any moisture on the plants to dry during the day, thereby lessening the risk of fungal disease. To avoid overwatering, check the amount of moisture in the rootzone by poking your finger into the top 1–2" of soil before applying any water.

To save time, money and water, consider installing an irrigation system. Irrigation systems apply water

Ornamental, yet functional sprinkler

Containers and baskets need regular watering.

exactly where it is needed, near the roots, and reduce the amount of water lost to evaporation. A simple irrigation system could involve laying soaker hoses around your garden beds under the mulch. Consult with your local garden centers or landscape professionals for more information.

Annuals in hanging baskets and planters will probably need to be watered more frequently than plants in the ground, especially during hot, dry weather. The smaller the container, the more often the plants will need watering. If the soil in your container dries out, water it several times to make sure water is absorbed throughout the planting medium.

Osteospermum performs well with weekly fertilizing.

Fertilizing

Many annuals will flower profusely if they are fertilized regularly. Some gardeners fertilize hanging baskets and container gardens every time they water, using a very diluted fertilizer so as not to burn the roots. Too much fertilizer, however, can result in weak plant growth that is susceptible to pest and disease problems. Some plants, such as nasturtiums, grow better without fertilizer and may produce few or no flowers when fertilized excessively.

Fertilizer comes in various forms. Liquids and water-soluble powders are the easiest to use when watering. Slow-release pellets or granules are mixed into the garden or potting soil or sprinkled around the plant and left to work through the summer.

Your local garden center should carry a good selection of fertilizers. Follow the directions on the containers carefully because using too much fertilizer can kill your plants by burning their roots. Organic fertilizers have an added benefit in that they feed the soil, not just the plants. Healthy soil allows plants to grow better over the course of the summer. Organic fertilizers don't work as quickly as many inorganic fertilizers, but often don't leach out as quickly. Organic fertilizers can be watered into soil or used as foliar sprays as often as weekly.

Organics also usually have lower nitrogen, phosphorus and potassium ratios than chemical fertilizers. Check labels for ingredients. Because of their lower nutrient ratios and ingredients from natural sources, organic fertilizers do not disrupt the microorganism balance in the soil to the same extent as chemical fertilizers.

Many organic fertilizer ingredients are available separately. Products to use on their own include bonemeal, liquid fish emulsion and alfalfa pellets, which contain triacontanol, a very powerful plant growth hormone that stimulates the roots to better use the fertilizer that is applied. You can also use synthetic phosphorus as a substitute for bonemeal.

Grooming

Good grooming helps keep your annuals healthy and neat, makes them flower more profusely and prevents many pest and disease problems. Grooming methods may include pinching, trimming, staking and deadheading.

Pinch out (remove by hand or with scissors) any straggly growth and the tips of leggy annuals. Plants in cell-packs may develop tall and straggly growth in an attempt to get light. Pinch back the long growth when transplanting to encourage bushier growth. Also remove any yellow or dying leaves.

Tall larkspurs may require staking.

If annuals appear tired and withered by mid-summer, try trimming them back by a quarter to a half to encourage a second bloom. Mounding or low-growing annuals, such as petunias, respond well to trimming. New growth will sprout along with a second flush of flowers. Fertilize plants lightly at this time.

Some annuals have very tall growth and cannot be pinched or trimmed. Instead, remove the main shoot after it blooms, and side shoots may develop.

Tall annuals, such as larkspur, may require staking with bamboo or other tall, thin stakes. Tie the plant loosely to the stake—strips of nylon hosiery make soft ties that won't cut into the plant. Make sure the strips are narrow so as not to show. Stake bushy plants with twiggy branches or tomato cages. Insert the twigs or cages around the plant when it is small, and it will grow to fill in and hide the supports.

Deadheading, or removing faded flowers, tidies plants and often helps prolong their bloom. It also helps keep annuals healthy because decaying flowers can harbor pests and diseases. Get into the habit of picking off spent flowers as you are looking around your garden. Some plants, such as impatiens and wax begonias, are self-cleaning or self-grooming, meaning that they drop their faded blossoms on their own.

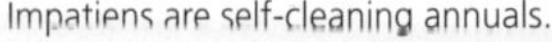

Impatiens are self-cleaning annuals.

Growing Perennials as Annuals

Many plants grown as annuals are actually perennials, such as geraniums, which are native to warm climates and are unable to survive our colder winters. Other plants grown as annuals are biennials, such as Canterbury bells, and are started very early in the year to allow them to grow and flower in a single season. These perennials and biennials are indicated as such in the plant entries. You can use several techniques to keep these plants for more than one summer.

Perennials with tuberous roots, such as dahlias, can be dug up in fall, after the plant dies back, and replanted in late winter or early spring. If there is a chance that the ground may freeze, dig up the tubers before that happens. Shake the loose dirt from the roots and let them dry in a cool dark place. Once they are dry, the rest of the soil should brush away. Dust the tubers with an antifungal powder, such as garden sulfur (found at garden centers), before storing them in moist peat moss or coarse sawdust. Keep them in a cool, dark, dry place that doesn't freeze. Check on them once a month, and lightly spray the storage medium with water if tubers appear very dry. If they start to sprout, pot them and keep them in moist soil in a bright window. They should be potted by latc winter or early spring so that they will be ready for planting in spring.

Cuttings can be taken from large or fast-growing plants such as black-eyed Susan vine. Grow late-summer cuttings over the winter for new spring plants. Cuttings are also a good idea for seed-grown plants that have developed unique foliage or other features not likely to be replicated with a new batch of seeds. See *Perennials for Minnesota and Wisconsin* for information on taking and growing cuttings.

Geranium is a perennial grown as an annual.

If winter storage sounds like too much work, replace your annuals each year and leave the hard work to the growers.

Canterbury bells is a biennial.

Problems & Pests

NEW ANNUALS ARE PLANTED IN THE GARDEN EACH SPRING, AND different species are often grown each year. These factors make it difficult for pests and diseases to find their preferred host plants and establish a population. On the other hand, because annual species are often grown together in masses, any problems that do set in over the summer may attack all the plants.

For many years pest control meant spraying or dusting to eliminate every pest in the landscape. A more moderate approach advocated today is known as IPM (Integrated Pest (or Plant) Management). The goal of IPM is to reduce pest problems to levels of damage acceptable to you. Consider whether the damage is localized or covers the entire plant. Will the damage kill the plant or only affect its outward appearance? Can the pest be controlled without chemicals? For an overview of IPM, you can consult the University of Minnesota website, <http://ipmworld.umn.edu/> or the University of Wisconsin website, <http://ipcm.wisc.edu/programs/school/default.htm>. IPM includes learning about your plants and the conditions they need for healthy growth, what pests might affect your plants, where and when to look for those pests and how to control them. Keep records of pest damage because your observations can reveal patterns useful in spotting recurring problems and in planning your maintenance regime.

An effective and responsible pest-management program has four steps. Cultural controls are the most important. Physical controls should be attempted next, followed by biological controls. Resort to chemical controls only when the first three possibilities have been exhausted.

Cultural controls are the gardening techniques you use daily. Growing annuals in the conditions they prefer and keeping soil healthy with plenty of organic matter are the best defenses against pests and diseases. Other cultural controls you can use include choosing varieties of annuals that are resistant to pests and problems; spacing your plants to ensure good air circulation around them and to reduce the stress of competing for light, nutrients and space; removing plants that are decimated by the same pests every year; disposing of diseased foliage and branches; and preventing the spread of disease by keeping gardening tools clean and tidying up fallen leaves and dead plant matter at the end of every growing season.

Physical controls are generally used to combat insect problems. An example of such a control is picking insects off plants by hand, easy if you catch the problem when it is just beginning. Large, slow insects such as Japanese beetles are particularly easy to pick off. Other physical controls include traps, barriers, scarecrows and natural repellents that make a plant taste or smell bad to pests. Garden centers offer a wide array of such devices. Physical control of diseases usually involves removing the infected plant or parts of the plant to keep the problem from spreading.

Biological controls make use of populations of natural predators. Such animals as birds, snakes, frogs, spiders, lady beetles and certain bacteria help keep pest populations at a manageable level. Encourage these creatures to take up permanent residence in your garden. A birdbath and birdfeeder will encourage birds to enjoy your yard and feed on a wide variety of insect pests. Many beneficial insects are probably already living in your garden, and you can encourage them to stay and multiply by planting appropriate food sources. For example, many beneficial insects eat nectar from flowers such as daisies and the perennial yarrow.

Another form of biological control is *B.t.* (the soil bacterium *Bacillus thuringiensis* var. *kurstaki*), which breaks down the gut lining of some insect pests. It is commonly available in garden centers.

Chemical controls should be used only as a last resort because they can do more harm than good. Chemical pesticide products can be either organic or synthetic. If you have tried cultural, physical and biological methods and still wish to take further action, call your local county Extension office to obtain a list of pesticides recommended for particular diseases or insects. Try to use organic types, available at most garden centers. Organic sprays are no less dangerous than synthetic ones, but they will at least break down into harmless compounds, often much sooner than synthetic compounds. Consumers are demanding effective pest products that do not harm the environment, so less toxic and more precisely targeted pesticides are becoming available. See also the environmentally friendly alternatives listed on p. 290.

Frogs eat many insect pests.

GLOSSARY OF PESTS & DISEASES

Anthracnose

Fungus. Yellow or brown spots on leaves; sunken lesions and blisters on stems; can kill plant.

What to Do: Choose resistant plants; keep soil well drained; thin out stems to improve air circulation; avoid handling wet foliage. Remove and destroy infected plant parts; clean up and destroy debris from infected plants at end of growing season. Liquid copper spray can prevent spread to other susceptible plants.

Aphids

Tiny, pear-shaped insects, winged or wingless; green, black, brown, red or gray. Cluster along stems, on buds and on leaves. Suck sap from plants; cause distorted or stunted growth. Sticky honeydew forms on surfaces and encourages sooty mold growth.

What to Do: Squish small colonies by hand; dislodge them with water spray; spray serious infestations with insecticidal soap, horticultural oil or neem oil; encourage predatory insects and birds that feed on aphids.

Aster Yellows

see Viruses

Beetles

Many types and sizes; usually rounded in shape with hard, shell-like outer wings covering membranous inner wings. Some are beneficial, e.g., ladybird beetles ('ladybugs'); others, e.g., Japanese beetles, flea beetles, blister beetles, leaf skeletonizers and weevils, eat plants. Larvae: see Borers, Grubs. Leave wide range of chewing damage: make small or large holes in or around margins of leaves; consume entire leaves or areas between leaf veins ('skeletonize'); may also chew holes in flowers.

What to Do: Pick beetles off at night and drop them into an old coffee can half filled with soapy water (soap prevents them from floating); spread an old sheet under plants and shake off beetles to collect and dispose of them. Use a hand-held vacuum cleaner to remove them from plant. Parasitic nematodes are effective if the beetle goes through part of its growing cycle in the ground.

Green aphids

Blight

Fungal or bacterial diseases, many types; e.g., leaf blight, snow blight, tip blight. Leaves, stems and flowers blacken, rot and die.

What to Do: Thin stems to improve air circulation; keep mulch away from base of plants; remove debris from garden at end of growing season. Remove and destroy infected plant parts. Use horticultural oil as a preventive measure. Compost tea is also effective.

Borers

Larvae of some moths, wasps, beetles; very damaging plant pests. Worm-like; vary in size and get bigger as they bore through plants. Burrow into stems, leaves and/or roots and rhizomes, destroying conducting tissue and weakening stems to cause breakage.

Leaves will wilt; may see tunnels in leaves, stems or roots; rhizomes may be hollowed out entirely or in part.
What to Do: May be able to squish borers within leaves. Remove and destroy bored parts; may need to dig up and destroy infected roots and rhizomes.

Bugs (True Bugs)

Small insects, up to 1/2" long; green, brown, black or brightly colored and patterned. Many beneficial; a few pests, such as lace bugs, pierce plants to suck out sap. Toxins may be injected that deform plants; sunken areas left where pierced; leaves rip as they grow; leaves, buds and new growth may be dwarfed and deformed.
What to Do: Always properly identify bugs before implementing controls. Remove debris and weeds from around plants in fall to destroy overwintering sites. Pick off by hand and drop into soapy water. Use parasitic nematodes if part of bug's growth cycle is in the ground. Spray plants with insecticidal soap or neem oil.

Canker

Swollen or sunken lesions, often on stems, caused by many different bacterial and fungal diseases. Most canker-causing diseases enter through wounds.
What to Do: Maintain plant vigor; avoid causing wounds; control borers and other tissue-dwelling pests. Prune out and destroy infected plant parts. Sterilize pruning tools before and after use.

Caterpillars

Larvae of butterflies, moths, sawflies. Include budworms, cutworms, leaf rollers, leaf tiers, loopers. Chew foliage and buds; can completely defoliate plant if infestation severe. May also eat flowers, new leaf growth, young plants and seedlings.
What to Do: Removal from plant is best control. Use high-pressure water and soap, or pick caterpillars off by hand. Use old toilet tissue rolls to make barrier collars around plant bases; push tubes at least halfway into ground. Control biologically using *B.t.*

Damping Off

see p. 30

Galls

Unusual swellings of plant tissues that may be caused by insects, such as *Hemerocallis* gall midge, or by diseases. Can affect leaves, buds, stems, flowers, fruit. Often a specific gall affects a single genus or species.
What to Do: Cut galls out of plant and destroy them. Galls caused by insects usually contain the insect's eggs and juvenile stages. Prevent such galls by controlling insects before they lay eggs; otherwise, try to remove and destroy infected tissue before young insects emerge. Generally insect galls more unsightly than damaging to plant. Galls caused by diseases often require destruction of plant. Avoid placing other plants susceptible to same disease in that location.

Lygus bug, a true bug, feeding on cosmos

Gray Mold (*Botrytis* Blight)

see Blight

Grubs

Larvae of different beetles, commonly found below soil level; usually curled in C-shape. Body white or gray; head may be white, gray, brown or reddish. Problematic in lawns; may feed on plant roots. Plant wilts despite regular watering; may pull easily out of ground in severe cases.

What to Do: Toss any grubs found while digging onto a stone path or patio for birds to devour; apply parasitic nematodes.

Leafhoppers & Treehoppers

Small, wedge-shaped insects; can be green, brown, gray or multi-colored. Jump around frantically when disturbed. Suck juice from plant leaves, cause distorted growth, carry diseases such as aster yellows.

What to Do: Encourage predators by planting nectar-producing plants. Wash insects off with strong spray of water; spray with insecticidal soap or neem oil.

Leaf Miners

Tiny, stubby larvae of some butterflies and moths; may be yellow or green. Tunnel within leaves leaving winding trails; tunneled areas lighter in color than rest of leaf. Unsightly rather than health risk to plant.

What to Do: Remove debris from area in fall to destroy overwintering sites; attract parasitic wasps with nectar plants. Remove and destroy infected foliage; can sometimes squish by hand within leaf. Floating row covers prevent eggs from being laid on plant. Bright blue sticky cards, available in most nurseries, attract and trap adult leaf miners.

Leaf miner damage

Leaf Spot (Leaf Blotch)

Two common types: one caused by bacteria and the other by fungi. *Bacterial:* small brown or purple speckles grow to encompass entire leaves; leaves may drop. *Fungal:* black, brown or yellow spots; leaves wither; e.g., scab, tar spot, leaf blotch.

What to Do: Bacterial infection more severe; must remove entire plant. For fungal infection, remove and destroy infected plant parts. Sterilize removal tools; avoid wetting foliage or touching wet foliage; remove and destroy debris at end of growing season. Spray plant with liquid copper. Compost tea or a mixture of baking soda and citrus oil also works in most instances.

Mealybugs

Tiny crawling insects related to aphids; appear to be covered with white fuzz or flour. More often found on houseplants than in the garden. Sucking damage stunts and stresses plant. Mealybugs excrete honeydew, promoting sooty mold.

What to Do: Remove by hand from smaller plants; wash off plant with soap and water; wipe off with alcohol-soaked swabs; remove heavily infested leaves; encourage or introduce natural predators such as mealybug destroyer beetle and parasitic wasps; spray with insecticidal soap. Note: larvae of mealybug destroyer beetle look like very large mealybugs.

Mildew

Two types, both caused by fungus, but with slightly different symptoms. *Downy mildew:* yellow spots on upper sides of leaves and downy fuzz on undersides; fuzz may be yellow, white or gray. *Powdery mildew:* white or gray powdery coating on leaf surfaces that doesn't brush off.

What to Do: Choose resistant cultivars; space plants well; thin stems to encourage air circulation; tidy any debris in fall. Remove and destroy infected leaves or other parts. Spray compost tea or highly diluted fish emulsion (1 tsp. per qt. of water) to control downy and powdery mildew. Control powdery mildew by spraying foliage with mixture of horticultural oil and baking soda in water. Three applications one week apart needed.

Mites

Tiny, eight-legged relatives of spiders. Examples: spider mites, rust mites, thread-footed mites. Invisible or nearly invisible to naked eye; red, yellow, green or translucent; usually found on undersides of plant leaves. Suck juice out of leaves; may see their fine webs on leaves and stems; may see mites moving on leaf undersides; leaves become discolored and speckled in appearance, then turn brown and shrivel up.

What to Do: Wash off with a strong spray of water daily until all signs of infestation are gone; predatory mites are available through garden centers; apply insecticidal soap, horticultural oil or neem oil.

Nematodes

Tiny worms that give plants disease symptoms. One type infects foliage and stems; the other infects roots. *Foliar:* yellow spots that turn brown on leaves; leaves shrivel and wither; problem starts on lowest leaves and works up plant. *Root-knot:* plant is stunted; may wilt; yellow spots on leaves; roots have tiny bumps or knots.

What to Do: Mulch soil, add organic matter, clean up debris in fall; don't touch wet foliage of infected plants. Can add parasitic nematodes to soil. Remove infected plants in extreme cases.

Rot

Several different fungi or bacteria that affect different parts of plant and can kill plant. *Bacterial soft rot:* enters through wounds; begins as small, water-soaked lesions on roots and leaves. As lesions grow, their surfaces darken but remain unbroken, while underlying tissue becomes soft and mushy. Lesions may ooze if surface broken. *Black rot:* bacterial; enters through pores or small wounds. Begins as V-shaped lesions along leaf margins. Leaf veins turn black and

Powdery mildew

eventually plant dies. *Crown rot (stem rot):* fungal; affects base of plant, causing stems to blacken and fall over and leaves to yellow and wilt. *Root rot:* fungal; leaves yellow and plant wilts; digging up plant shows roots rotted away.
What to Do: Keep soil well drained; don't damage plant when digging around it; keep mulches away from plant base. Remove infected plants.

Rust

Fungi. Pale spots on upper leaf surfaces; orange, fuzzy or dusty spots on leaf undersides. Examples: blister rust, hollyhock rust, white rust.
What to Do: Choose varieties and cultivars resistant to rust; avoid handling wet leaves; provide plant with good air circulation; use horticultural oil to protect new foliage; clean up garden debris at end of season. Remove and destroy infected plant parts. Do not put infected plants in compost pile.

Scale Insects

Tiny, shelled insects that suck sap, weakening and possibly killing plant or making it vulnerable to other problems. Scale appears as tiny bumps typically along stems or on undersides of foliage. Once female scale insect has pierced plant with mouthpart, it is there for life. Juvenile scale insects are called crawlers.

Slug

What to Do: Wipe off with alcohol-soaked swabs; spray with water to dislodge crawlers; prune out heavily infested branches; encourage natural predators and parasites; spray horticultural oil in spring before bud break.

Slugs & Snails

Both mollusks. Snails have a spiral shell, slugs lack shells; both have slimy, smooth skin. Can be up to 8" long; gray, green, black, beige, yellow or spotted. Leave large ragged holes in leaves and silvery slime trails on and around plants.
What to Do: Remove slug habitat including garden debris or mulches around plant bases. Use slug-repellent mulches. Increase air circulation. Pick off by hand in the evening and squish with boot or drop in can of soapy water. Spread diatomaceous earth (available in garden centers; do not use the kind meant for swimming pool filters) on soil around plants to pierce and dehydrate the soft slug or snail bodies. Commercial slug and snail baits are effective; some new formulations nontoxic to pets and children. Stale beer in a sunken, shallow dish may be effective. Attach strips of copper to wood around raised beds or to small boards inserted around susceptible groups of plants; slugs and snails get shocked if they touch copper surfaces.

Smut

Fungus that affects any above-ground plant parts including leaves, stems and flowers. Forms fleshy white galls that turn black and powdery.
What to Do: Remove and destroy infected plants. Avoid placing same plants in that spot for next few years.

Sooty Mold

Fungus. Thin black film forms on leaf surfaces and reduces amount of light getting to leaf surfaces.
What to Do: Wipe mold off leaf surfaces; control insects such as aphids, mealybugs, whiteflies (honeydew left on leaves encourages mold).

Thrips

Tiny insects, difficult to see; may be visible if you disturb them by blowing gently on an infested flower. Yellow, black or brown with narrow, fringed wings. Suck juice out of plant cells, particularly in flowers and buds, causing gray-mottled petals and leaves, dying buds and distorted, stunted growth.
What to Do: Remove and destroy infected plant parts; encourage native predatory insects with nectar plants; spray severe infestations with insecticidal soap or with horticultural oil. Use blue sticky cards to attract and trap adults.

Viruses

Plant may be stunted and leaves and flowers distorted, streaked or discolored. Examples: aster yellows, mosaic virus, ringspot virus.
What to Do: Viral diseases in plants cannot be treated. Destroy infected plants; control insects such as aphids, leafhoppers and whiteflies that spread disease.

Whiteflies

Tiny, white, moth-like insects that flutter up into the air when the plant is disturbed. Live on undersides of leaves and suck juice out, causing yellowed leaves and weakened plants; leave sticky honeydew on leaves, encouraging sooty mold.
What to Do: Usual and most effective remedy is to remove infested plant so insects don't spread to rest of garden. Destroy weeds where insects may live. Attract native predatory beetles and parasitic wasps with nectar plants. Spray severe cases with insecticidal soap. Use yellow sticky cards or make your own sticky trap: mount tin can on stake, wrap can with yellow paper and cover with clear small plastic bag smeared with petroleum jelly; replace bag when full of flies. Plant sweet alyssum in immediate area. Make a spray from old coffee grounds.

Wilt

If watering hasn't helped a wilted plant, one of two wilt fungi may be at fault. *Fusarium wilt:* plant wilts, leaves turn yellow then die; symptoms generally appear first on one part of plant before spreading to other parts. *Verticillium wilt:* plant wilts; leaves curl up at edges; leaves turn yellow then drop off; plant may die.
What to Do: Both wilts difficult to control. Choose resistant plant varieties and cultivars; clean up debris at end of growing season. Destroy infected plants; solarize (sterilize) soil before replanting—contact local garden center for assistance.

Worms

see Caterpillars, Nematodes

Mosaic virus

ABOUT THIS GUIDE

THE ANNUALS IN THIS BOOK ARE ORGANIZED ALPHABETICALLY BY their most familiar common names, which in some cases is the proper botanical name. The botanical name is always listed (in italics). Readers are strongly encouraged to learn these botanical names. Common names are sometimes spread over any number of very different plants. They also change from region to region. The additional common names that appear after the primary reference illustrate this. Only the true, botanical name for a plant defines exactly what plant it is, everywhere on the planet. Learning and using the botanical names for plants you grow allows you to discuss, research and purchase plants with supreme confidence and satisfaction.

Clearly indicated at the beginning of each entry are height and spread ranges, which encompass the measurements for all recommended species and varieties, along with the full range of flower colors for these plants. At the back of the book, the Quick Reference Chart summarizes different features and requirements of the annuals; you will find this chart handy when planning for diversity in your garden.

Each entry gives clear instructions and tips for seeding, planting and growing the annual, and it recommends some of our favorite species and varieties. Keep in mind that many more hybrids, cultivars and varieties are often available than we have space to mention. Check with your local greenhouses or garden centers when making your selection. There are many annuals we have not included in this book that are available and we encourage you to explore. That said, we have ensured that there are plenty of wonderful annuals in this book to provide you with many seasons of gardening pleasure.

Pests or diseases that commonly affect an annual, if any, are also listed for each entry. Consult the 'Problems & Pests' section of the introduction for information on how to solve these problems.

Finally, we have kept jargon to a minimum, but check the glossary on p. 288 for any unfamiliar terms.

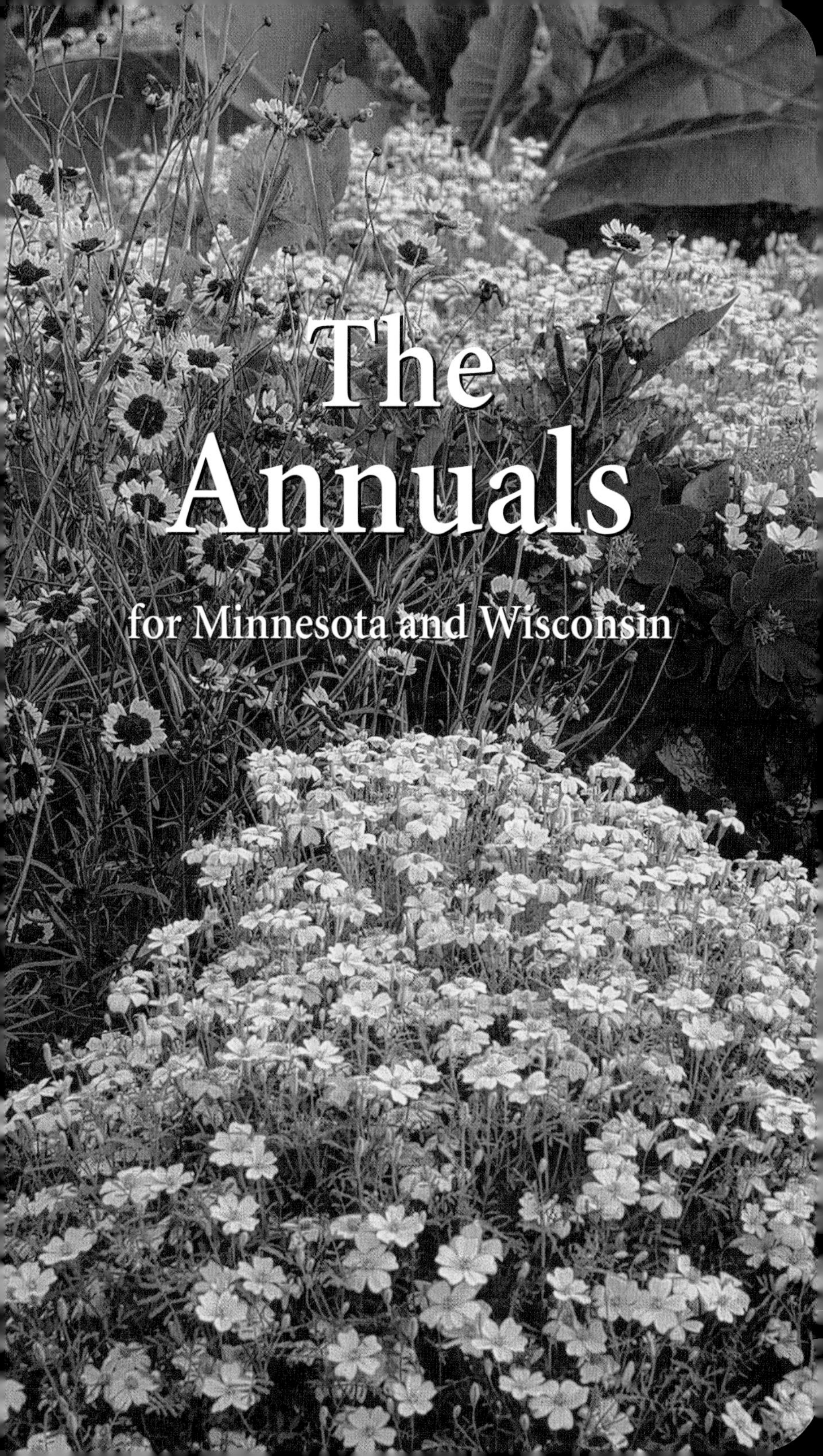
The
Annuals
for Minnesota and Wisconsin

Ageratum

Floss Flower

Ageratum

Height: 6–36" **Spread:** 10–14" **Flower color:** blue, purple, white, pink, burgundy

WITH THEIR SOFT, GLOBULAR, FUZZY BLOOMS AND OFTEN diminutive size, ageratums are one of the all-time most popular edging plants. Perfect for the very front of the mixed annual/perennial border while equally arresting in flower boxes, pots and planters, they provide long-lasting color with a minimum of fuss. Newer, taller varieties such as 'Red Sea' remind us that the gardening world is ever-changing; ageratums aren't just for the front of the garden anymore!

Planting

Seeding: Indoors in early spring, or direct sow after last frost. Don't cover the seeds, because they need light to germinate.

Planting out: Once soil has warmed

Spacing: 4–12"

Growing

Ageratum prefers **full sun** but tolerates partial shade. The soil should be **fertile, moist** and **well drained**. This plant doesn't like to have its soil dry out; a moisture-retaining mulch will cut down on how frequently you have to water. Don't mulch too thickly or too close to the base of the plant, or it may develop crown rot or root rot. Adequate fertilization is required to keep ageratum blooming throughout the summer.

Though the plant needs deadheading to keep it flowering, the blossoms are extraordinarily long-lived, making

'Shell Pink Hawaii'

The genus name Ageratum *comes from the Greek for 'without age,' a reference to the long-lasting flowers. The specific epithet* houstonianum *refers not to the Texas city but to William Houston, who collected the flowers in Mexico and the Antilles.*

'Blue Hawaii'

'Blue Horizon' (above), 'Blue Hawaii' (below)

ageratum an easy-care plant for sunny gardens. Removing the spent flowers will keep this plant looking good all summer.

To dry ageratum flowers for crafts and floral arrangements, cut fresh flowers in the morning, bundle them together with rubber bands and hang them upside down in a location with good air circulation.

Tips

The smaller varieties, which become almost completely covered with the fluffy flowerheads, make excellent edging plants for flowerbeds. They are also attractive grouped in masses or grown in planters. The taller varieties are useful in the center of a flowerbed and make interesting cut flowers.

Recommended

A. houstonianum forms a large, leggy mound up to 24" tall. Clusters of fuzzy blue, white or pink flowers are held above the foliage. Many cultivars are available; most have been developed to maintain a low, compact form that is more useful in the border. **Artist Hybrids** are compact, mounding plants 8–12" tall, with plentiful flowers. They have been bred to continue flowering throughout the summer, always overgrowing the old dead flowers with new blooms. 'Artist Alto Blue' grows 14–18" tall and 12–14" wide. It has the same excellent summer-long performance as the shorter Artist varieties. 'Artist Blue' has true blue flowers. 'Artist Purple' bears bright purple or plum-colored flowers. **'Bavaria'** grows about 10" tall, with blue and white bicolored flowers. **'Blue Hawaii'** is a compact plant 6–12" tall, with blue flowers. **'Blue Horizon'** is an upright cultivar with lavender blue flowers. It grows 24–36" tall. **'Leilani'** ('Leilani Blue') is a vigorous, densely mounding plant growing 14–16" tall and 10–12" wide. It produces sky blue flowers. **'Red Sea'** grows to 20" tall and bears burgundy red to wine red flowers. Pinching this cultivar encourages strong branching. **'Shell Pink Hawaii'** has light pink double flowers on compact 6–12" tall plants.

'Blue Hawaii' (photos this page)

Problems & Pests

Powdery mildew may become a problem. Be sure to plant ageratum in a location with good air circulation to help prevent fungal diseases.

Amaranth

Amaranthus

Height: 3–5' **Spread:** 12–30" **Flower color:** red, yellow, green; flowers inconspicuous in some species grown for foliage.

FAST ON THE HEELS OF THE TREND toward tropicals comes a renewed interest in amaranth, which is flat-out one of the strangest-looking plants known to botany. Growing the plants requires a little forethought, for it's difficult to place them with more common garden flowers and not have them look like some aberrant invasion. One sure bet is to feature one plant in one container, placed as a focal point in a grouping of containers. In the garden, amaranth can be stunning, but it's best if the garden also features tropicals such as angel's trumpet (*Datura*, *Brugmansia*), cape fuchsia (*Phygelius*) and *Dracaena*, now available in a growing number of northern nurseries.

In ancient Greece, amaranth was regarded as a symbol of fidelity and immortality. The flowers were used to decorate tombs.

Planting

Seeding: Indoors about three weeks before last frost; direct sow once soil has warmed

Planting out: Once soil has warmed

Spacing: 12–24"

Growing

A location in **full sun** is preferable. The soil should be **poor to average** and **well drained.** Don't give these plants rich soil or overfertilize them, or their growth will be tall, soft and prone to falling over. Joseph's coat will also lose some of its leaf color when overfertilized; its colors are more brilliant in poorer soil.

Seeds started indoors should be planted in peat pots or pellets to avoid disturbing the roots when transplanting.

Love-lies-bleeding self-seeds and can show up year after year. Unwanted plants are easy to uproot when they are young.

A. caudatus 'Viridis'

Amaranth has astringent properties and is used by herbalists to stop bleeding and to treat diarrhea.

A. tricolor 'Illumination'

A. caudatus (above), A. caudatus cultivar (below)

Tips

Love-lies-bleeding is attractive grouped in borders and in mixed containers, where it requires very little care or water over summer.

Joseph's coat is a bright and striking plant that is best used as an annual specimen in a small group rather than in a large mass planting, where it quickly becomes overwhelming. It is also attractive mixed with large-leaved plants in the back of a border. It can self-sow in abundance, so remove unwanted seedlings in early summer to prevent them from over-taking the garden.

Recommended

A. caudatus (love-lies-bleeding) has erect stems and long, drooping, rope-like, fluffy red, yellow or green flower spikes that can be air dried. The plant grows 3–5' tall and 18–30" wide. **'Love Lies Bleeding'** has blood red flowers. **'Viridis'** has bright green flowers.

A. tricolor (Joseph's coat) is a bushy, upright plant with brightly colored foliage and inconspicuous flowers. It may grow up to 5' tall and 12–24" wide if started early indoors. If directly sown in the garden, it grows 18–24" tall and about 12" wide. The cultivars are only a little smaller than the species. The foliage is variegated and can be green, red, bronze, chocolate-purple, orange, yellow or gold. **'Aurora'** has bright to creamy yellow upper foliage and dark green lower foliage. **'Illumination'** has hanging foliage in crimson and gold. It grows 4' tall and 12" wide. **'Joseph's Coat'** has green, scarlet and cream foliage.

Problems & Pests

Cold nights below 50° F will cause leaf drop. Rust, leaf spot, root rot, aphids and some viral diseases are potential problems.

A. caudatus 'Love Lies Bleeding'

Several species of amaranth are used as cooking herbs and vegetables because their leaves are high in protein.

A. tricolor 'Joseph's Coat'

Angel's Trumpet

Datura, Trumpet Flower

Brugmansia, Datura

Height: 22"–10' **Spread:** 1–6' **Flower color:** white, yellow, pink, purple

IF IT'S HEIGHT AND GIRTH YOU'RE after, angel's trumpet fits the bill. Large, trumpet-shaped flowers in a variety of colors are heavily perfumed, most noticeably in the evening. Angel's trumpets are actually shrubby perennials grown as annuals across much of the United States. They look great trained to a stake or small trellis in larger containers and are easy to overwinter indoors. Beware, however, that all parts of these plants, especially the seeds, contain alkaloids that if ingested can cause liver damage, neurotoxicity and death. Never include them in a landscape or home open to small children and pets.

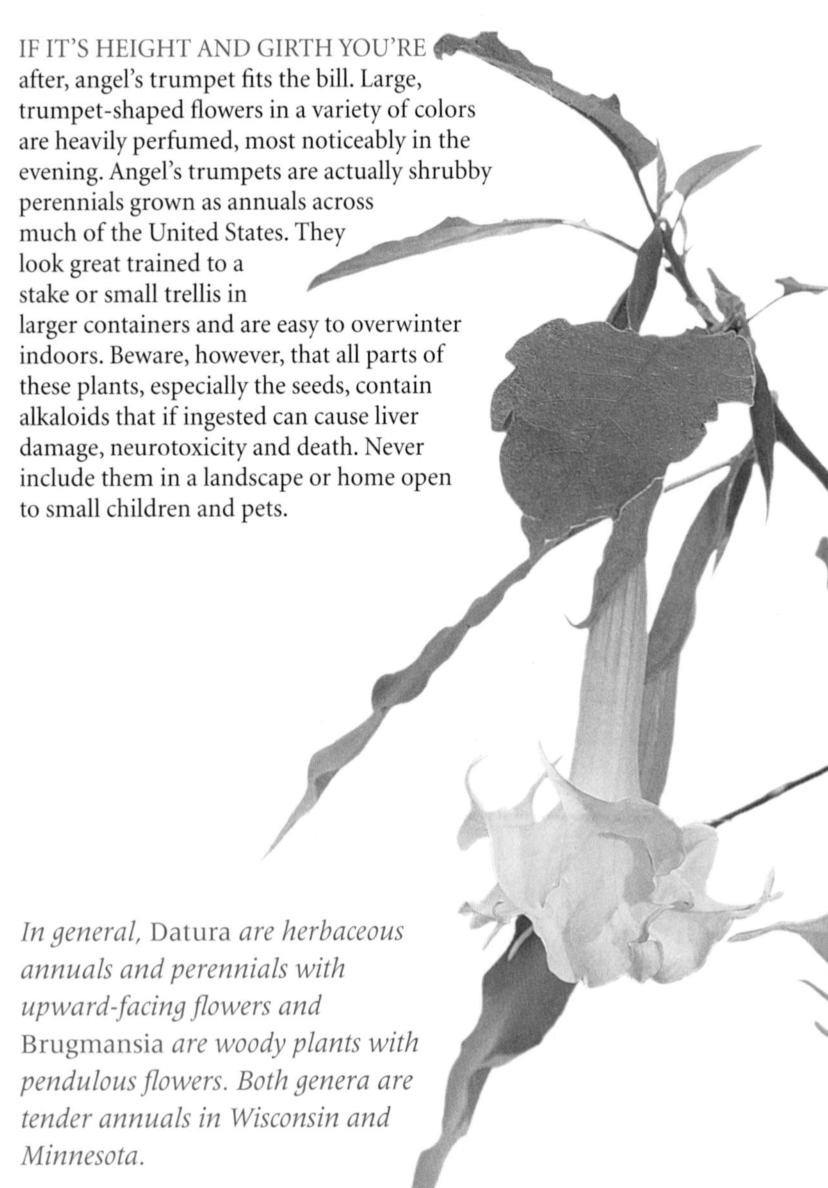

In general, Datura *are herbaceous annuals and perennials with upward-facing flowers and* Brugmansia *are woody plants with pendulous flowers. Both genera are tender annuals in Wisconsin and Minnesota.*

Planting

Seeding: Slow to germinate, may not grow to flowering size until late summer. Start indoors in midwinter. *Datura* self-sow.

Planting out: Once soil has warmed and frost danger has passed

Spacing: 24–36"

Growing

All angel's trumpets prefer **full sun**. The soil should be **fertile, moist** and **well drained.** Don't allow plants to dry out completely, particularly during hot, dry weather. Plants recover quickly from wilting when watered. Angel's trumpet really hates to dry out and thrives on very high fertility. A weekly feeding is recommended.

The popularity of angel's trumpets has increased in recent years, and many garden centers carry started plants. Cuttings taken in autumn will root quickly and can be overwintered in a sunny window. They'll be ready to plant outside early the next summer.

B. 'Charles Grimaldi'

The American Brugmansia and Datura Society notes that the flower colors and forms of these plants can be affected by temperature, pH levels, nutrition, humidity, stress, sun and shade.

D. metel

B. candida

Tips

Angel's trumpet flowers tend to open at night. Grow these plants where you will be able to enjoy their intoxicating scent in the evening—near a patio or in a large container on a deck. If angel's trumpets are planted under an open window, the scent will carry into the room. These plants are attractive as specimens or in groups.

Angel's trumpet plants become large quickly and create a tropical look on a patio or deck. Use a heavy pot because they easily become top-heavy and tip over.

Recommended

B. candida is a woody plant that can be grown in a bright room indoors in winter and moved outdoors in summer. In a container it rarely grows over 10'. Trim it back to keep it the size you want. It bears fragrant, white, trumpet-shaped flowers that may open only at night. **'Double Blackcurrant Swirl'** produces double lilac flowers with frilled margins. **'Ecuador'** bears double white flowers. **'Grand Marnier'** has apricot yellow flowers. **'Lemon Yellow'** produces an abundance of large, lemon yellow flowers. **'Shredded White'** bears unique double flowers with loosely bunched, white petals.

***B.* 'Charles Grimaldi'** is another woody plant. The large, funnel-shaped, pendulous flowers are a beautiful, luminous orange-yellow. This is an excellent container plant for a patio or deck. In a container it rarely grows over 10'.

***B.* 'Dr. Seuss'** ('Hetty Krauss') grows to about the same size as 'Charles Grimaldi.' The yellow-orange flowers are deeper yellow and have a wider flare. The American Brugmansia and Datura Society states that 'Dr. Seuss' is a parent of 'Charles Grimaldi.' 'Dr. Seuss' performs well in our northern climate.

D.* x *hybrida (*B.* x *hybrida*) includes several hybrid plants of uncertain parentage. **'Angel's Trumpets'** ('Angel') bears white flowers edged with pale pink. The hybrids in the **Queen Series** are commonly available, often offered in seed catalogs. 'Golden Queen' is a cultivar in this series that grows 3–4$^1/_2$' tall and bears yellow double flowers.

D. innoxia (*D. meteloides;* downy thorn apple) is a small, tender perennial grown as an annual. It grows 36" tall and, if allowed, can sprawl to

5–6'. The flowers are white, pink or lavender. **Subsp. *quinquecuspida*** ('Missouri Marble') grows 22" tall and 24" wide. The upright flowers are cream colored with wide flares tinged sky blue; they are attractive to butterflies.

D. metel (horn of plenty, jimsonweed, locoweed) is an annual that easily self-seeds. It grows to 12–36" tall and wide. The species produces single flowers, but many double- and even triple-flowered cultivars are available. **'Cornucopia'** has double purple and white flowers.

Problems & Pests

Problems with whiteflies, spider mites and mealybugs are possible, though more likely on plants grown indoors.

Angel's trumpets are in the same family (Solanaceae) *as tomatoes, potatoes, peppers and nightshade plants.*

D. metel 'Cornucopia'

Annual Chrysanthemum

Chrysanthemum, Painted Daisy

Chrysanthemum

Height: 18–36" **Spread:** 10–24" **Flower color:** white, red, yellow, purple, multi-colored

ANNUAL CHRYSANTHEMUMS ARE ESSENTIALLY THOSE PLANTS comprising the large proportion of the *Chrysanthemum* family that are not frost-hardy. Many varieties resemble the hardy mums we grow (or attempt to grow) as perennials, as well they should. However, annual varieties have the additional quality of an extended bloom time, in some instances from early summer to fall. Like all mums, they benefit from spring pinching, which will result in stockier plants and heavier blooms.

Planting

Seeding: Direct sow or sow seed indoors in spring

Planting out: Late February to mid-April

Spacing: 10–18"

Growing

Annual chrysanthemums prefer **full sun** but tolerate partial shade. The soil should be of **average fertility** and **well drained.** A second sowing in mid-summer will bring late-season flowers. Deadhead to prolong the blooming period.

Tips

Annual chrysanthemums are brightly colored additions to the informal bed or border. These sturdy plants can help support tall plants that often require staking.

Recommended

C. carinatum (tricolor chrysanthemum, painted daisy) is an upright plant that grows about 24–36" tall and 18–24" wide and blooms from late summer to fall. The most common flower colors are red, yellow, white or purple; the centers, petal bases and petal tips are often banded in different colors. **'Court Jesters'** has many colors, with the petal bases banded in orange or red. **Rainbow Series** has many colors, with two bands at the petal bases.

C. coronarium (crown daisy) is a tall, upright plant with ferny foliage. It grows up to 36" tall and spreads up to 18". Single, yellow flowers are borne from late spring to mid-summer. **'Primrose Gem'** bears bright yellow flowers on compact plants that are half the size of the species.

Problems & Pests

Aphids love these flowers and should be washed off with insecticidal soap or a brisk spray from the garden hose.

C. carinatum (photos this page)

Annual chrysanthemums make long-lasting and popular cut flowers. In Victorian flower symbolism, a white chrysanthemum represents truth and a yellow chrysanthemum indicates slighted love.

Annual Phlox

Phlox

Height: 6–18" **Spread:** 8–10" or more **Flower color:** purple, pink, red, blue, white, yellow

GROW ANNUAL PHLOX AND YOU'LL SOON FIND SPOTS FOR IT everywhere, for this showy, easy-to-grow bedding staple adapts to a wide variety of uses. Mass any number of varieties in a large bed for a colorful quilt that blooms from mid-summer into fall, or use it as an edging plant in formal gardens. Its compact, bushy growth makes it a nice addition to rock gardens, and its ability to flourish in the dog days of summer adds value to all manner of container plantings.

Planting

Seeding: Direct sow in early spring and mid-summer

Planting out: Around the last frost date

Spacing: 6–8"

Growing

Annual phlox prefers **full sun**. The soil should be **fertile, moist** and **well drained.** This plant is easily grown from seed. Germination takes 10–15 days. It can be propagated from cuttings and will root easily in moist soil. Plants can be spaced quite closely together. Deadhead to promote blooming.

Take care when transplanting into the garden as the roots are said to resent disturbance. Seed into peat pots or pellets or into large cell-packs. Do not butterfly the roots when planting.

Tips

Use annual phlox on rock walls and in beds, borders, containers and rock gardens.

Recommended

P. drummondii forms a bushy plant 6–18" tall and 10" or more in spread. It bears clusters of white, purple, pink or red flowers. **21st Century Series** are vigorous, heat-tolerant, compact plants with great lateral branching. Abundant flowers come in a range of blue, crimson, magenta, salmon, scarlet and white. Plants grow 10" tall and 8–10" wide. **'Coral Reef'** bears attractive pastel-colored flowers. **Twinkle Mixed** includes compact plants 8" tall, with unusual small, star-shaped flowers. The colors of the petal margins and centers often contrast with the main petal color.

Problems & Pests

To avoid fungal problems, provide good drainage and don't let water stand on the leaves late in the day. Water the plants in the morning during dry spells and avoid handling wet foliage.

P. drummondii (above and below)

This Texan species of phlox is named for Thomas Drummond (1790–1835), who collected plants in North America.

Baby Blue-Eyes

Five Spot

Nemophila

Height: 6–12" **Spread:** 12" **Flower color:** blue, white, purple

MY INTEREST IN ANNUALS DEFINITELY TOOK A GIANT LEAP forward the first time I spotted baby blue-eyes *(N. menziesii)* in a neighbor's garden. It was massed in a sunny corner, heavenly blue-and-white clouds of blooms billowing out on both sides of a split-rail fence. It remains one of my favorite annuals, particularly because it flowers freely in my partially sunny yard. *N. maculata* is more of a novelty plant, with evenly spaced, purple blotches on the tip of each petal.

Planting

Seeding: Direct sow around last frost date

Planting out: If necessary, after last frost date

Spacing: 8–12"

Growing

Baby blue-eyes grows well in **full sun** or **partial shade.** The soil should be **fertile, moist** and **well drained.** Avoid letting the soil dry out completely. Shelter these plants from strong winds and avoid placing them near paths, where the tender foliage may be damaged by passersby.

These plants resent being transplanted and should be sown directly into the garden. They can be started indoors in peat pots or pellets in early spring if desired.

Tips

These plants can be used as annual groundcovers or as edging for borders. They work well in mixed planters, hanging baskets and window boxes.

Recommended

N. maculata (five-spot) is a low, mound-forming plant. It grows up to 12" tall, with an equal spread. The white flowers have purple veins, and each of the five petals has a single purple spot at the tip, giving the plant its common name.

N. menziesii (baby blue-eyes) is a low, spreading plant 6–10" tall and 12" wide. The flowers are blue with white centers. **Subsp. *atomaria*** ('Snowstorm') has slightly off-white flowers spotted purple-black. **'Pennie Black'** has very dark purple flowers with silvery white edges.

Problems & Pests

Aphids and powdery mildew can cause problems.

'Pennie Black' (photos this page)

These plants may cease flowering during the hottest part of summer if they are allowed to completely dry out.

Baby's Breath

Gypsophila

Height: 12–36" **Spread:** 12–24" **Flower color:** white, pink, purple

OFFERING A BROADER RANGE OF BOTH BLOOM SIZE AND COLOR than perennial *Gypsophila*, annual baby's breath is a superb flower for both garden and container use. *G. muralis* most closely approximates the light and airy look of the perennial. The relatively large, bright white flowers of 'Covent Garden' are striking both in daytime and evening, when they positively glow in moonlight. The only bad news is you need to dumb down your gardening instincts to grow baby's breath well. Don't amend the soil around the plant, and let the soil dry out between waterings.

Planting

Seeding: Indoors in late winter; direct sow from mid-spring to early summer

Planting out: Mid-spring

Spacing: 8–18"

Growing

Baby's breath grows best in **full sun**. The soil should be of **poor fertility, light, sandy** and **alkaline**. These plants are drought tolerant and do not grow well in wet soil. Space seedlings closer together because slightly crowded plants flower more profusely.

Tips

Their clouds of flowers make baby's breath ideal for rock gardens, rock walls, mixed containers or borders with bold-colored flowers. Pinch back or shear occasionally to encourage reblooming. Baby's breath plants will reseed.

Recommended

G. elegans forms an upright 12–24" mound of airy stems, foliage and flowers. The flowers are usually white but may have pink or purple veining that gives them a colored tinge. **'Carminea'** has deep carmine rose flowers. **'Covent Garden'** has very large, white flowers and grows 20–36" tall. **'Red Cloud'** produces carmine to pink flowers. **'Rosea'** has pale rose pink flowers.

G. muralis grows 12–18" tall and 12–20" wide and has dense, dark green foliage and flower clusters held above the foliage. **'Garden Bride'** grows 12" tall and bears double or semi-double pink flowers. **'Gypsy,'** a 1997 All-America Selections winner, grows 12–14" tall and bears semi-double to double pink flowers.

Problems & Pests

Infrequent problems with fungal diseases can be avoided by not over-watering and not handling plants when they are wet. Leafhoppers can infect plants with aster yellows.

G. elegans cultivar (above), *G. elegans* (below)

Bachelor's Buttons

Cornflower

Centaurea

Height: 12–39" **Spread:** 6–24" **Flower color:** blue, violet, red, maroon, pink, white

THIS OLD-TIME FAVORITE—YOUR GREAT-GRANDMOTHER COULD well have grown it—remains a popular and highly desirable annual today. Blooming from early summer into fall, it's great for large areas and makes a smashing annual addition to naturalized prairie or meadow plantings. Do you have a sunny ditch or long stretch of road that you'd like to seed and forget? Combine bachelor's buttons with California poppy and hound's tongue *(Cynoglossum)* for a traffic-stopping display.

Planting

Seeding: Direct sow in mid-spring or start indoors in late winter

Planting out: Around last frost

Spacing: 12"

Growing

Bachelor's buttons grow well in **full sun to partial shade** with shade in the afternoon. **Fertile, moist, well-drained** soil is preferable, but any soil is tolerated. Light frost won't harm these plants.

Start seeds in peat pots or pellets to avoid disturbing roots during transplanting. Shear spent flowers and old foliage in mid-summer for fresh new growth. Deadheading prolongs blooming.

Tips

Bachelor's buttons are great filler plants in a mixed border or wildflower or cottage-style garden. Mix them with other plants—as the bachelor's buttons fade, the other plants can fill in the space they leave. They make good cut flowers and can also be dried.

Recommended

C. cyanus is an upright annual that grows 12–36" tall and spreads 6–24". The flowers are most often blue but can also be shades of red, pink, violet or white. **'Black Gem'** ('Black Ball,' 'Black Boy') has dark maroon, ruffled blooms above silvery foliage. It grows 18–30" tall. Plants in the **'Boy Series'** grow up to 39" tall and have large double flowers in many colors. **'Florence Series'** includes compact, dwarf cultivars 12–18" tall, with flowers in various colors. **'Frosty Mixed'** grows 24–30" tall. It bears white flowers edged with pink or pastel flowers in blue, pink, rose, deep red and maroon, all edged with frosty white.

Problems & Pests

Aphids, downy mildew and powdery mildew may cause problems.

C. cyanus (photos this page)

The name bachelor's buttons originated in Victorian times, when these blossoms were worn as inexpensive boutonnieres. Today, a bachelor's button is a button attached with a wire, so it doesn't need to be sewn on.

Begonia

Begonia

Height: 6–24" **Spread:** 6–24" **Flower color:** pink, white, red, yellow, orange, bicolored or picotee; plant also grown for foliage

BEGONIA ENCOMPASSES A LARGE FAMILY OF WONDERFUL, versatile plants. Wax begonias are the most common bedding annuals and work well when massed. The bronze foliage of the Cocktail hybrids is particularly attractive when mixed randomly throughout green-leaved varieties. Rex begonias arrived on the scene only recently, sporting magnificent foliage with dark tones highlighted by purple, pink, silver and green variegation. They are terrific for shaking up the usual look of the semi-shady woodland garden, and they are wonderful alternatives to coleus for container planting.

Planting

Seeding: Indoors in early winter

Planting out: Once soil has warmed

Spacing: 6–20", according to spread of variety

Growing

Light or **partial shade** is best although some wax begonias tolerate sun if their soil is kept moist. The soil should be **fertile,** rich in **organic matter** and **well drained** with a **neutral to acidic pH.** Allow the soil to dry out slightly between waterings, particularly for tuberous begonias. Begonias like warm weather, so don't plant them before the soil warms in spring. If they sit in cold soil, they may become stunted.

Begonias can be tricky to grow from seed. The tiny seeds can be mixed with a small quantity of fine sand before sowing to ensure a more even distribution of seeds. Keep the soil surface moist but not soggy, and do not cover the seeds. Maintain daytime temperatures at 70°–80° F and night temperatures above 50° F.

B. x tuberhybrida pendula

Rex begonias can also be grown as houseplants, and in that form the leaves take on different colors depending on the levels of light.

B. semperflorens Cocktail Series

B. x *hybrida* Dragon Wing

B. x *tuberhybrida pendula*

Begonias can be potted individually once they have three or four leaves and are large enough to handle.

Tubers can be purchased in early spring and started indoors. Plant them with the concave side up. The tubers of tuberous begonias can also be uprooted when the foliage dies back and stored in slightly moistened peat moss over winter. The tubers will sprout new shoots in late winter and can be potted for the following season.

Wax begonias can be dug out of the garden before the first frost and grown as houseplants in winter in a bright room.

Tips

All begonias are useful for shaded garden beds and planters. The trailing tuberous varieties can be used in hanging baskets and along rock walls where the flowers will cascade over the edges. Wax begonias have a neat, rounded habit that makes them particularly attractive as edging plants. They can also be paired with roses and geraniums in a front-yard bed for a formal look. Creative gardeners are using rex begonias, with their dramatic foliage, as specimen plants in containers and beds.

Recommended

B. x *hybrida* Dragon Wing is a trade name for a variety with deep scarlet to deep pink flowers and angel-winged foliage. This plant grows 12–15" tall and 15–18" wide, and it is heat tolerant.

B. **Rex Cultorum Hybrids** (rex begonias) is a group of plants developed from crosses between *B. rex* and other species. They grow 6–12" tall and 12–16" wide. Rex begonias are grown for their dramatic, colorful foliage and are especially stunning planted among hostas in the shade garden. The **Great American Cities**

B. semperflorens in boxwood hedge

B. Rex 'New York Swirl'

B. x *tuberhybrida* cultivar

Wax begonias are ideal flowers for lazy gardeners because they are generally pest free and bloom all summer, even without deadheading.

B. Rex Cultorum hybrid

Series from Proven Winners has wild, dark color combinations, including the following selections: **'Chicago Fire'** foliage features magenta centers deepening to near-black edges; **'Denver Lace'** has pointed silver, pink, purple and green leaves; **'Maui Mist'** has dark pink foliage sprinkled with silver; and **'New York Swirl'** produces large leaves with silvery pink centers and margins and purple veins.

B. semperflorens (wax begonias) have pink, white, red or bicolored flowers and green, bronze, reddish or white-variegated foliage. The plants are 6–14" tall and 6–24" wide. Plants in the **Ambassador Series** are heat tolerant and have dark green leaves and white, pink or red flowers. **Cocktail Series** plants are sun and heat tolerant. They have bronzed leaves and red, pink or white flowers. **Harmony Series** plants grow 6–8" tall and 8–10" wide. Plants in this companion series to the Prelude Series have bronze foliage and pink, scarlet or white flowers. **Maestro Series** plants are 6–12" tall with green and bronze foliage and white, pink and red flowers. **Prelude Series** plants reach 6–8" in height and 8–10" in spread and have green foliage with coral, pink, scarlet, rose, white or bicolored flowers. **'Queen Red'** is a vigorous grower bearing fully double, rose-like, red flowers. **Senator Series** begonias are very similar to the Ambassador Series but have bronze foliage. Plants in the **Victory Series** grow 8–10" tall with green or bronze foliage. The flowers come in pink or red shades and can also be white or bicolored.

B.* x *tuberhybrida (tuberous begonias) are generally sold as tubers. The flowers come in many shades of red, pink, yellow, orange or white. They can also be picotee, with the petal margins colored differently than the rest of the petal. The plants grow 8–24" tall and wide. **Charisma Series** plants tolerate heat and rain and grow 12" tall and wide. They produce 2 1/2" wide, double flowers in pink, salmon orange, scarlet or deep rose. **Non-stop Series** begonias can be started from seed. They grow about 12" tall and wide; their double and semi-double flowers come in pink, yellow, orange, red or white. ***B.* x *t. pendula*** includes attractive pendulous begonias with flowers in many bright shades. **Illumination Series** is a cascading type of *B.* x *t. pendula* for baskets and other container plantings. Different varieties have flowers in white, salmon, apricot, scarlet or rose on plants 18–20" tall.

Problems & Pests

Problems with stem rot and gray mold can result from overwatering.

B. x *tuberhybrida* cultivar

Begonias have attractive, colorful foliage. Use the dark-leaved forms of wax begonias for splashes of contrasting color next to a gray-leaved licorice plant (Helichrysum) *or silver dead nettle* (Lamium).

B. semperflorens with ageratum

Black-Eyed Susan

Coneflower, Gloriosa Daisy

Rudbeckia

Height: 8–36" or more **Spread:** 12–20" **Flower color:** yellow, orange, red, brown or sometimes bicolored; brown or green centers

IT'S HARD TO NAME A BETTER ANNUAL THAN *RUDBECKIA* FOR providing dynamic color from mid-summer to frost. Like its perennial sibling, annual *Rudbeckia* features large, often bicolored flowers with attractive, cone-like central disks. 'Gloriosa' holds its own against all comers when placed in the middle to the back of the mixed annual/perennial garden bed while the shorter cultivars listed here jazz up the front of the border as well as larger patio pots.

Planting

Seeding: Indoors in late winter; direct sow in mid-spring

Planting out: Late spring

Spacing: 12–18"

Growing

Black-eyed Susan grows equally well in **full sun** or **partial shade**. The soil should be of **average fertility, humus rich, moist** and **well drained**. This plant tolerates heavy clay soil and hot weather. If it is growing in loose, moist soil, black-eyed Susan may reseed itself. Keep cutting the flowers to promote more blooming.

Tips

Black-eyed Susan can be planted individually or in groups. Use it in beds and borders, large containers, meadow plantings and wildflower gardens. This plant blooms well even in the hottest part of the garden.

'Prairie Sun'

Black-eyed Susan cut flowers are long lasting in arrangements.

'Becky'

'Irish Eyes' with verbascum

R. hirta is a perennial that is grown as an annual. It is not worth trying to keep over winter because it grows and flowers quickly from seed.

Recommended

R. hirta forms a bristly mound of foliage 12–36" tall and 12–18" wide. It bears bright yellow, daisy-like flowers with brown centers in summer and fall. **'Becky'** is a dwarf cultivar up to 12" tall, with large flowers in solid and mixed shades of yellow, orange, red and brown. **'Cherokee Sunset'** bears 3–4$\frac{1}{2}$" semi-double and double flowers in yellow, orange, brown and red. **'Gloriosa'** bears 6" wide flowers in solid or bicolored shades of yellow, orange, bronze and gold. Plants grow to 36" tall. **'Indian Summer'** has huge flowers, 6–10" across, on sturdy stems 36" tall or taller. **'Irish Eyes'** grows up to 30" tall and has green-centered single flowers. **'Prairie Sun'** grows 36" tall

'Gloriosa'

and 20" wide. Its yellow flowers are 4" in diameter and have distinctive green centers. **'Sonora'** grows 16–20" tall and bears 5" wide, bicolored flowers with mahogany red towards the base of the petals and bright gold towards the tips. **'Toto'** is a dwarf cultivar that grows 8–18" tall, small enough for planters.

Problems & Pests

Good air circulation will help prevent fungal diseases such as powdery mildew, downy mildew and rust. Aphids can occasionally cause problems.

The genus Rudbeckia *includes annual, biennial and perennial species, all native to North America.*

'Irish Eyes' (above), *R. hirta* (below)

Black-Eyed Susan Vine

Thunbergia

Height: 5' or more **Spread:** equal to height, if trained **Flower color:** yellow, orange, violet blue or white, usually with dark centers

THIS ADAPTABLE AFRICAN NATIVE IS BECOMING INCREASINGLY popular as gardeners continue to seek out attractive vining plants for walls, trellises, posts and arbors. The very showy orange flowers are distinctive for the dark purple throat. Note, too, the importance of knowing this plant's botanical name *(Thunbergia)*. Although this annual vine goes by the common name black-eyed Susan vine, it is in no way related to black-eyed Susan *(Rudbeckia)*. Both plants do share the ability to grow quickly and brighten a spot with their sunny flowers.

Planting

Seeding: Indoors in mid-winter; direct sow in mid-spring

Planting out: Late spring

Spacing: 12–18"

Growing

Black-eyed Susan vines grow well in **full sun, partial shade** or **light shade**. Grow in **fertile, moist, well-drained** soil that is high in **organic matter**. Keep the soil evenly moist.

Tips

Black-eyed Susan vines can be trained to twine up and around fences, walls, trees and shrubs. They are also attractive trailing down from the top of a rock garden or rock wall or growing in mixed containers and hanging baskets.

These vines are perennials treated as annuals. They can be quite vigorous and may need to be trimmed back from time to time, particularly if they are brought inside for winter. To acclimatize the plants to the lower light levels indoors, gradually move them to more shaded locations. Keep in a bright room out of direct sunlight for winter. The following spring, harden off the plants before moving them outdoors.

Recommended

T. alata is a vigorous, twining climber with yellow flowers. **'Alba'** has white flowers. The commonly available **Susie Series** bears large flowers in yellow, orange or white.

T. grandiflora (skyflower, sky vine, blue trumpet vine, clock vine) is also a twining climber but bears stunning, pale violet blue flowers. It takes far longer to come into flower than does *T. alata*—look for the 3" blooms in late summer or fall.

T. alata cultivars (photos this page)

Fashion wire frames into any shape to grow your vine into whimsical topiary.

Browallia

Amethyst Flower

Browallia

Height: 6–18" **Spread:** up to 8–18" **Flower color:** purple, blue, white

ONE MIGHT SAY THAT EVERY PLANT LISTED IN THIS BOOK HAS pretty flowers; ugly flowers don't survive long in the nursery trade. Browallia is a plant with a beauty that tends to get noticed by visitors. It is certainly helped in this regard by dark blue, softly lobed flowers held in great abundance above clean, attractively veined foliage. 'White Troll' turns the same trick, only with heavenly, snow white blooms. I use browallia heavily in containers and flower boxes, and I am always amazed to find such a magnificent beauty flowering so freely in my less-than-full-sun yard.

Planting

Seeding: Indoors in late winter

Planting out: Once soil has warmed

Spacing: 8–10"

Growing

Browallia tolerates any light conditions from **full sun to full shade,** but flower production and color are best in partial shade. The soil should be **fertile** and **well drained.** Do not cover the seeds when seeding, because they need light to germinate. They do not like the cold, so wait several weeks after the last frost before setting out the plants. Pinch tips often to encourage new growth and more blooms.

Tips

Grow browallia in mixed borders, mixed containers or hanging baskets.

Browallia can be brought indoors at the end of the season to be used as a houseplant during winter. It can also be grown as a houseplant all year.

Recommended

B. speciosa forms a bushy mound of foliage. This plant grows 8–18" tall, with an equal or narrower spread, and bears white, blue or purple flowers all summer. **'Garden Leader Blue'** has deep blue flowers on plants that grow 6–12" tall and 10–14" wide. **Jingle Bells hybrids** include 'Blue Bells,' 'Jingle Bells Mix' and 'Silver Bells,' which vary from 8–12" in both height and spread. **'Starlight'** forms a compact mound up to 8" tall and wide. Its flowers may be light blue, bright blue, purple or white. The **Troll Series** includes 'Blue Troll' and 'White Troll,' which are compact and bushy. They grow about 10" tall.

Problems & Pests

Browallia is generally problem free. Whiteflies may cause some trouble.

'White Troll'

Browallia was named by the great botanist Linnaeus for his contemporary John Browall (1707–55), a Swedish bishop and botanist.

B. speciosa

Calendula

Pot Marigold, English Marigold

Calendula

Height: 10–24" **Spread:** 8–20" **Flower color:** cream, yellow, gold, orange, apricot

IF IT'S COLOR YOU'RE AFTER—COLOR THAT CAN BE SEEN A BLOCK away—you'll enjoy a long relationship with calendula. One of the easiest to grow annuals, calendula blooms from early summer right up until killing frost. Anytime you're dealing with big, robust flowers, I think it's a good idea to plant a swath of five or more plants because one calendula sitting there looking fabulous is only going to scream for more. These plants make excellent cut flowers and work well zig-zagging through cottage gardens and large, informal beds.

Planting

Seeding: Direct sow in mid-spring; sow indoors a month or so earlier

Planting out: Mid-spring

Spacing: 8–10"

Growing

Calendula does equally well in **full sun** or **partial shade**. It likes cool weather and can withstand a light frost. The soil should be of **average fertility** and **well drained**. Young plants are sometimes hard to find in nurseries. Calendula is easy to start from seed and that is how most gardeners grow it. A second sowing in mid-summer gives a good fall display. Deadhead to prolong blooming and keep plants neat.

Tips

This informal plant looks attractive in borders and mixed into the vegetable patch. It can also be used in mixed planters. Calendula is a cold-hardy annual and often continues flowering until the ground freezes completely.

Recommended

C. officinalis is a vigorous, tough, upright plant 12–24" tall, with a slightly lesser spread. It bears daisy-like single flowers in shades from yellow to orange. Cultivars can have single or double flowers in a wide range of yellow and orange shades. **'Bon Bon'** is a dwarf plant that grows 10–12" tall and comes in all available colors. **'Fiesta Gitana'** ('Gypsy Festival') is a dwarf plant that bears flowers in a wide range of colors. **'Pacific Beauty'** grows about 18" tall. It bears large flowers in varied colors. **'Pink Surprise'** bears pale orange and apricot flowers tinged with pink.

C. officinalis cultivar

Problems & Pests

Infrequent problems with aphids, whiteflies, powdery mildew and fungal leaf spot can occur. Plants often perform well even when afflicted with such problems.

C. officinalis

California Poppy

Eschscholzia

Height: 8–18" **Spread:** 8–18" **Flower color:** orange, yellow, red; less commonly pink, cream

CALIFORNIA POPPIES EXHIBIT A RELAXED, DELICATE CHARM THAT'S perfect for cottage gardens and larger, informal planting areas. The arching, blue-green stems and fine foliage contrast wonderfully with both the flower form and color. The fact that it isn't fussy about soil and re-seeds freely makes it perfect for large, sunny areas you'd like to naturalize instead of mow.

The petals of California poppy are edible and brighten up an everyday salad.

Planting

Seeding: Direct sow in early to mid-spring

Spacing: 6–12"

Growing

California poppy prefers **full sun**. The soil should be of **poor to average fertility** and **well drained**. With too rich a soil, the growth will be lush and green, but the plants will bear few, if any, flowers. This plant is drought tolerant once established and flowering.

Never start this plant indoors because it dislikes having its roots disturbed. California poppy will sprout quickly when planted directly in the garden. Sow in early spring for blooms in summer.

California poppy requires a lot of water for germination and development of young plants. Until they flower, provide the plants with regular and frequent watering.

Tips

California poppy can be included in an annual border or annual planting in a cottage garden. This plant self-seeds wherever it is planted; it is perfect for naturalizing in a meadow garden or rock garden where it will come back year after year.

Recommended

E. californica grows 8–18" tall and wide, forming a mound of delicate, feathery, blue-green foliage. It bears satiny orange or yellow flowers all summer. **'Apricot Flambeau'** has creamy yellow, lightly orange-tinged, fluted petals with bright orange markings. **'Ballerina'** has a mixture of colors and semi-double or double

E. californica (photos this page)

flowers. **'Chiffon'** forms compact plants, up to 8" tall, that bear semi-double flowers in pink and apricot. **'Mission Bells'** bears ruffled, double and semi-double flowers in mixed and solid shades of orange, yellow, red, cream and pink. **'Thai Silk'** bears flowers in pink, red, yellow and orange with silky, wavy-edged petals. The compact plants grow 8–10" tall.

Problems & Pests

California poppy generally has few pest problems, but fungi may cause trouble occasionally.

Candytuft

Iberis

Height: 6–12" **Spread:** 8" or more **Flower color:** white, pink, purple, red

CANDYTUFTS ARE INVALUABLE FOR BRINGING SOFT, SOOTHING color to semi-shady portions of the yard and garden. Though they do well in full sun, I use them as a refreshing alternative to impatiens in dappled shade. They are difficult to find in nurseries as transplants but are readily available as seed.

If your candytuft seems to be blooming less often as summer progresses, trim it back lightly to promote new growth and more flowers.

Planting

Seeding: Indoors in late winter; outdoors around last frost

Planting out: After last frost

Spacing: 6"

Growing

Candytuft prefers to grow in **full sun** or **partial shade**. Partial shade is best if it gets very hot in your garden. Like many species in the mustard family, candytuft dislikes heat; blooming will often slow down or decrease in July and August. The soil should be of **poor** or **average fertility, well drained** and have a **neutral** or **alkaline pH**.

Deadheading when the seeds begin to form will keep candytuft blooming, but do let some plants go to seed to guarantee repeat performances.

Tips

This informal plant can be used on rock walls, in mixed containers or as edging for beds.

Recommended

I. umbellata (globe candytuft) has flowers in shades of pink, purple, red or white. The plant grows 6–12" tall and spreads 8" or more. **'Dwarf Fairy'** ('Dwarf Fairyland') is a compact plant that bears many flowers in a variety of pastel shades. **'Flash Mix'** grows to 12" tall and bears flowers in deep red, bright purple and white. 'Red Flash' is part of the series and has bright red flowers.

Problems & Pests

Keep an eye open for slugs and snails. Caterpillars can also be a problem. In poorly drained soil, fungal problems may develop.

Canterbury Bells

Cup-and-Saucer Plant

Campanula

Height: 18–36" **Spread:** 12" **Flower color:** blue, purple, pink, white

TALL ANNUALS THAT RISE ABOVE 24" ARE HIGHLY DESIRABLE BUT are the exception rather than the rule. Good height is just one of the worthy attributes of breezy and bold Canterbury bells, a staple of the traditional cottage garden for generations. With rich, true blue flowers and heights up to 36", this plant always stands out. The color range of various cultivars includes pink, white and purple, giving you plenty of design options. Since most varieties cease blooming at summer's end, it's best to plant Canterbury bells where they will be hidden by other plants come fall.

Planting

Seeding: Indoors in mid-winter

Planting out: Early spring

Spacing: 6–12"

Growing

Canterbury bells prefers **full sun** but tolerates partial shade. The soil should be **fertile, moist** and **well drained**. This plant will not suffer if the weather cools or if there is a light frost.

When sowing, leave seeds uncovered because they require light for germination. Harden off seedlings in a cold frame or on a sheltered porch before planting out. Canterbury bells transplants easily, even when in full bloom. Canterbury bells is actually a biennial treated as an annual, so plants must be started early in the year. Plants purchased in $3^1/_2$" pots may be too small to grow to flowering size the first year.

Tips

Planted in small groups, Canterbury bells looks lovely in a border or rock garden. It also makes a good addition to a cottage garden or other informal garden where its habit of self-seeding can keep it popping up year after year. The tallest varieties produce good flowers for cutting. Use dwarf varieties in planters.

Recommended

C. medium is a biennial treated as an annual that forms a basal rosette of foliage. The pink, blue, white or purple cup-shaped flowers are borne on tall spikes. The species grows 24–36" high and spreads about 12". **'Bells of Holland'** grows about 18" tall. It has flowers in various colors.

C. medium (photos this page)

'Champion' is a true annual cultivar, flowering much sooner from seed than the species or many other cultivars. Blue or pink flowers are available. **'Russian Pink'** is an heirloom plant that is another true annual cultivar. It bears light pink flowers.

Problems & Pests

Occasional problems with aphids, crown rot, leaf spot, powdery mildew and rust.

Cape Marigold

Dimorphotheca

Height: 12–18" **Spread:** 18" **Flower color:** white, orange, yellow, pink or red; often with black, brown, orange, yellow or purple centers

CAPE MARIGOLDS SIZZLE IN THE GARDEN, THEIR LONG, CURVING petals of orange, apricot, salmon and red possessing a varnished sheen matched by few blooming plants. 'Glistening White' features pure white blooms with attractive golden eyes. They are stunning grouped in both formal and informal garden beds and borders and superb in cut flower arrangements. Their long bloom time and erect habit make them a good choice for large containers as well. A magnificent annual all the way around.

Planting

Seeding: Indoors in early spring; direct sow after last frost

Planting out: After last frost

Spacing: 12"

Growing

Cape marigolds like **full sun**. The soil should be **light, fertile** and **well drained**. These plants are drought resistant.

If growing cape marigolds from seed, water the young seedlings freely. Otherwise they will fail to thrive.

Cape marigolds do not grow well in rainy weather. Plant them under the eaves of the house, in window boxes or in raised beds to protect them from too much rain.

Tips

Cape marigolds are most attractive when planted in groups or masses. Use them in beds and borders. The flowers close at night and on cloudy days, so although they can be cut for flower arrangements, they might close if the vase isn't getting enough light.

Recommended

D. pluvialis (cape marigold; rain daisy) has white flowers with purple on the undersides and bases of the petals. **'Glistening White'** is a compact plant that bears large, pure white flowers with black centers.

D. x **'Salmon Queen'** bears salmon and apricot pink flowers on plants that spread to about 18".

D. sinuata (star of the veldt) forms a 12–18" mound. It bears yellow, orange, white or pink daisy-like flowers all summer. Cultivars with larger flowers are available.

D. x **'Starshine'** is a low, mound-forming cultivar with shiny flowers in pink, orange, white or red, with yellow centers.

D. pluvialis

Problems & Pests

Fungal problems are likely to occur in hot and wet locations. Dry, cool places produce healthy plants that are less susceptible to disease.

D. sinuata

Celosia
Cockscomb, Woolflower
Celosia

Height: 6"–4' **Spread:** equal to or slightly less than height
Flower color: red, orange, gold, yellow, pink, purple

THE FIERY PLUMES OF CELOSIA HAVE BEEN A FAVORITE OF MINE since I began gardening, and as newer and improved varieties have come on the scene, I appreciate the plant even more. Varieties of the Plumosa Group exhibit the plumes of dense flowers most often seen at nurseries. Combine red and orange varieties with a smattering of yellows, and it appears the ground is on fire. Plants in the Cristata Group have mounding blooms that resemble brain matter and are arresting used as edging in large containers or in combination with tropical plants such as amaranth.

Planting

Seeding: Indoors in late winter; direct sow in late spring

Planting out: Once soil has warmed

Spacing: 6–18", according to spread of variety

Growing

A sheltered spot in **full sun** is best. The soil should be **fertile and well drained**, with plenty of **organic matter** worked in. Celosia likes to be watered regularly.

Celosia grows best when directly sown in the garden. If you need to start it indoors, start the seeds in peat pots or pellets and plant them into the garden before they begin to flower. This also applies to nursery-purchased plants. If left too long in pots, celosia will suffer stunted growth and won't be able to adapt to the garden. Keep seeds moist while they are germinating and do not cover them.

Cristata Group cultivar, petunias, Plumosa Group cultivar behind

To dry the colorful plumes, pick the flowers when they are at their peak and hang them upside down in a cool, shaded place.

Plumosa Group 'Fairy Fountains'

C. spicata 'Startrek'

Plumosa Group cultivar

Tips

Celosia works well in borders and beds as well as planters. The flowers make interesting additions to arrangements, either fresh or dried.

A mass planting of plume celosia looks bright and cheerful in the garden. The popular crested varieties work well as accents and as cut flowers.

Recommended

C. argentea is the species from which both the crested and plume-type cultivars have been developed. The species itself is never grown. **Cristata Group** (crested celosia) has blooms that resemble brains or rooster combs. This group has many varieties and cultivars. **'Amigo Mix'** are compact plants 6–12" tall and 4–8" wide. The flowers come in a range of red, pink, orange and yellow and bloom from late spring to the first frost. **'Brain Mix Tall'** grows 3–4' tall and has flowers in several colors. **'Fireglow'** has brilliant red combs 6" across on plants 12–18" tall. **'Jewel Box'** bears flowers in red, pink, orange, yellow and gold on compact plants 10" tall. **Plumosa Group** (plume celosia) has feathery, plume-like blooms. This group also has many varieties and cultivars. **Castle Series** includes uniform, well-branched plants 12–16" tall and 8–12" wide, with dense flower clusters. 'Orange Castle' has orange flowers; 'Scarlet Castle' has scarlet red flowers. **Century Series** has neat, much-branched plants up to 24" tall and 18" in spread, with flowers in many bright colors. **'Fairy Fountains'** is a compact plant, 12" tall, that bears long-lasting flowers in red, yellow and pink.

C. spicata (*C. argentea* Spicata Group; wheat celosia) grows 10–18" tall and produces spike-like clusters of pink to rose flowers, often with a metallic sheen. **'Flamingo Feather'** grows 24–36" tall and has slender spikes of pink to white flowers. **'Flamingo Purple'** is bushier and taller with purple-white flower spikes and dark red-green stems and leaves. It grows about 36" tall. Another interesting recent development from the species is **'Startrek,'** which has bright pink flowers that radiate out from a central spike.

Problems & Pests

Celosia may develop root rot if planted out too early or if overwatered when first planted. Cool, wet weather is the biggest problem.

Cristata Group cultivar

The genus name Celosia *is derived from the Greek* keleos, *'burning,' referring to the intensely colorful blooms.*

Plumosa Group cultivar in large show bed

China Aster

Callistephus

Height: 6–36" **Spread:** 10–18" **Flower color:** purple, blue, pink, red, white, peach, yellow

I REFER TO CHINA ASTER AS "THE CHAMELEON PLANT"—depending on the variety, blooms may resemble those of peonies, chrysanthemums or daisies. Yet they are all China asters, sure to brighten up any sunny spot with their big, showy blooms. Like so many annuals that start flowering in mid-summer, China asters stand tall and assured in August, when many annuals have succumbed to the heat. Just don't forget to give them ample water!

Planting

Seeding: Indoors in late winter; direct sow after last frost

Planting out: Once soil has warmed

Spacing: 6–12"

Growing

China aster prefers **full sun** but tolerates partial shade. The soil should be **fertile, evenly moist, well drained** and of **neutral or alkaline pH.** China asters are heavy feeders. Fertilize often for best flower performance.

Start seeds in peat pots or peat pellets because this plant doesn't like having its roots disturbed. China aster has shallow roots that dry out quickly during dry spells; mulch to conserve moisture.

C. chinensis (photos this page)

Tips

The flowers of China aster put on a bright display when planted in groups. There are three height groups: dwarf, medium and tall. Use the dwarf and medium varieties as edging plants and the taller varieties for cut-flower arrangements. Tall varieties may require staking.

Problems & Pests

Wilt diseases and aster yellows can be prevented by planting China aster in different locations each year and by planting resistant varieties. Keep China aster away from calendula, which hosts potentially harmful insects and diseases.

Recommended

C. chinensis is the source of many varieties and cultivars. **'Comet'** is an early-flowering cultivar, growing about 10" tall, with large, quilled double flowers in white, yellow, pink, purple, red or blue. **'Duchess'** plants are wilt resistant. The sturdy stems, up to 24" tall, bear colorful flowers with petals that curve in towards the center. **'Meteor'** has plants up to 36" tall. The large flowers, up to 4" across, are bright red with yellow centers. **'Pot 'n' Patio'** is a popular dwarf cultivar that has double flowers and grows 6–8" tall, with an equal spread. **'Princess'** grows up to 24" tall and bears quilled, double or semi-double flowers in a wide range of colors.

Cleome

Spider Flower

Cleome

Height: 10"–5' **Spread:** 18–36" **Flower color:** pink, rose, violet, white

NORTHERN GARDENERS CAUGHT ON LONG AGO TO THE SPECIAL allure and charm of cleome, and it remains highly visible in gardens across Wisconsin and Minnesota. What's not to like? Among the tallest annuals easily grown in the north, this showy South American native towers above the competition while rarely requiring staking (though it's wise to keep it away from windy situations). Tall cleome looks best massed in groups of five or more plants, though the shorter varieties listed below look great in smaller clumps and in mixed container plantings.

Planting

Seeding: Indoors in late winter; direct sow in spring. Chill seeds overnight before planting.

Planting out: After last frost

Spacing: 12–30"

Growing

Cleome prefers **full sun** but tolerate partial shade. Any kind of soil will do fine. Mix in plenty of **organic matter** to help the soil retain moisture. These plants are drought tolerant, but they look and perform better if watered regularly. Don't water excessively or they will become leggy.

Deadhead to prolong the blooming period and to minimize these plants' prolific self-sowing. Self-sowed seedlings will start coming up almost as soon as the seeds hit the ground and can become invasive. Fortunately, the new plants are very distinctive and can be spotted poking up where they don't belong, making them easy

'Sparkler Blush'

'Hummingbird flower' might be a more appropriate name for these plants. They bloom through to fall, providing nectar for the tiny birds after many other flowers have finished blooming.

Royal Queen Series

C. hassleriana

C. hassleriana with flowering tobacco, geranium and impatiens

to pull up while they are still young. Flowers of self-sowed seedlings will most likely revert to light purple, the original species' color.

Tips

Cleome can be planted in groups at the back of a border. These plants are also effective in the center of an island bed. Use lower-growing plants around the edges to hide the leafless lower stems of the cleome.

Try adding the seedpods to dried arrangements.

Recommended

C. hassleriana is a tall, upright plant with strong, supple, thorny stems. It grows up to 5' tall. The foliage and flowers of this plant have a strong, but not unpleasant, scent. **'Helen Campbell'** has white flowers. **Royal Queen Series** has flowers in all colors, available by individual color or as a mixture of all available colors. The varieties are named by their color, e.g., 'Cherry Queen,' 'Rose Queen' and 'Violet Queen.' Plants in this series resist fading. **'Sparkler Blush'** is smaller than the species, growing up to 36" tall. It bears pink flowers that fade to white. This cultivar was an All-America Selections winner for 2002.

C. 'Linde Armstrong' is a compact, thornless variety, growing 10–18" tall and bearing rosy pink blooms most of the summer. It is very heat tolerant and well suited to container growing.

The flowers can be cut for fresh arrangements although the plants have an unusual smell that is very noticeable up close.

C. serrulata (Rocky Mountain bee plant) is native to western North America. It is rarely available commercially, but the dwarf cultivar **'Solo'** can be purchased and grown from seed. 'Solo' grows 12–18" tall and bears 2–3", pink and white blooms. This plant is thornless.

Problems & Pests

Aphids may be a problem.

Be careful when handling these plants because they have nasty barbs along the stems.

'Helen Campbell' (above), *C. hassleriana* (below)

Coleus

Solenostemon (Coleus)

Height: 6–36" or more **Spread:** usually equal to height **Flower color:** light purple; plant grown for multi-colored foliage

TO THE TOO-SHORT LIST OF ANNUALS FOR SHADE, GARDENERS are grateful to include coleus, one of the most valuable annuals available for those less-than-sunny spots. Coleus is grown for its marvelous foliage—the leaves are the show—and over the years new hybrids have expanded the palette to include a stunning rainbow of colors and patterns. Newer varieties listed below flourish in full sun, but I find the many tried-and-true, shade-loving specimens far and away the most useful for adding exotic color and texture to woodland plantings, pots, flower boxes and other containers placed in shade.

Planting

Seeding: Indoors in winter

Planting out: Once soil has warmed

Spacing: 8–12"

Growing

Seed-grown coleus prefers to grow in **light** or **partial shade**, but it tolerates full shade if the shade isn't too dense and full sun if the plants are watered regularly. Cultivars propagated from cuttings thrive in **full sun to partial shade**. The soil for all coleus should be of **high to average fertility, humus rich, moist** and **well drained**.

Place the seeds in a refrigerator for one or two days before planting them on the soil surface. Low temperatures will assist in breaking their dormancy. They need light to germinate. Seedlings will be green at first, but leaf variegation will develop as the plants mature. As your seedlings develop, decide which ones you like best, and when they are about three pairs of leaves high, pinch off the tip. The plants will begin to branch out.

'Life Lime'

Although coleus is a member of the mint family, with its characteristic square stems, it lacks the enjoyable culinary or aromatic qualities.

Wizard Series

Wizard Series (above)

Repeated pinching will create a very bushy plant.

Coleus is easy to propagate from stem cuttings, and in doing so you can ensure that you have a group of plants with the same leaf markings, shapes or colors. The cuttings should be about three leaf pairs long. Make the cut just below a leaf pair, and then remove the two bottom leaves. Plant the cuttings in pots filled with a soil mix intended for starting seeds. Keep the soil moist but not soggy. The plants should develop roots within a couple of weeks.

Coleus can be trained to grow into a standard (tree) form by pinching off the side branches as they grow. Once the plant reaches the desired height, pinch from the top.

Tips

The bold, colorful foliage creates a dramatic display in beds and borders. Coleus can also be used in mixed containers and as an edging plant. It can be grown indoors as a houseplant in a bright room.

Pinch off flower buds when they develop because the plants tend to stretch out and become less attractive after they flower.

Recommended

S. scutellarioides (*Coleus blumei* var. *verschaffeltii*) forms a bushy mound of foliage. The leaf edges range from slightly toothed to very ruffled. The leaves are usually multi-colored with shades ranging from pale greenish yellow to deep purple-black. The size may be 6–36", depending on the cultivar, and the spread is usually equal to the height. Hundreds of cultivars are available. The leaves of plants in the **Dragon Series** have bright yellow-green margins around multi colored centers.

Ducksfoot Series plants are fully sun-tolerant plants with flat leaves that resemble duck feet. This series includes **'Ducksfoot Red'** with glowing burgundy foliage; **'Indian Frills'** with purple- and pink-tinged green foliage; **'Midnight'** with very dark purple to black foliage; and **'Super Ducksfoot'** with large, burgundy-specked yellow and rose leaves.

'Garnet Robe' has a cascading habit and dark wine-red leaves edged with yellow-green. **'Molten Lava'** bears foliage with burgundy red centers and flaming red, lightly scalloped margins. **'Palisandra'** features velvety, purple-black foliage. **'Scarlet Poncho'** has wine red leaves edged with chartreuse. The **Wizard Series** includes compact plants with heart-shaped leaves.

Sun-loving varieties grown from cuttings include **'Alabama Sunset'** with spectacular orange, red and yellow leaves; **'Dark Star'** with dark, rich purple-black, scalloped leaves; **'Kingswood Torch'** with large, lovely, rich red leaves edged in dark purple; and **'Life Lime,'** a large, gold-leaved variety with occasional splashes of maroon.

Problems & Pests

Mealybugs, scale insects, aphids and whiteflies can cause trouble.

Ducksfoot Series (below)

Coreopsis
Tickseed
Coreopsis

Height: 18"–4' **Spread:** up to 18" **Flower color:** yellow, red, orange, brown

COREOPSIS IS A CHIPPER, FESTIVE ADDITION TO ANY GARDEN OR container, flourishing in dry, hot summers and still blooming well into fall. While the foliage brings nothing to the party, the plant blooms so profusely that the leaves are barely noticeable. Coreopsis isn't bothered by pollution, making it a great choice for city plots.

Planting

Seeding: Indoors in mid-winter; direct sow after last frost

Planting out: After last frost

Spacing: 8–12"

Growing

Coreopsis plants prefer **full sun**. The soil should be of **average to high fertility, light** and **well drained**. Poor soil is also tolerated but flowering is reduced. Good drainage is the most important factor for these drought-tolerant plants.

Tips

These annuals look comfortable growing in front of a rustic wooden fence or repeating in clusters in perennial beds. They make a beautiful color combination planted with deep purple coral bells or royal purple heliotrope. Well suited to naturalized meadow plantings, coreopsis can also be used in informal beds and borders, where they will flower all season if deadheaded regularly. These plants make lovely cut flowers.

Coreopsis plants can be blown over or have their stems broken during heavy rain or high winds. Twiggy branches, inserted while the plants are small, will give the plants a support structure to grow up into. In very windy spots, it is best to use the dwarf forms of coreopsis, such as 'Mardi Gras.'

Recommended

C. grandiflora is a clump-forming plant, 18–36" tall and about 18" wide. It bears bright yellow single flowers all summer. **'Early Sunrise,'** an All-America Selections winner, bears bright yellow double flowers on compact plants about 18" tall.

C. tinctoria (photos this page)

C. tinctoria forms a clump of basal leaves and tall, branching stems with just a few leaves. It grows up to 4' tall and spreads up to 18". The flowers are usually bright yellow with dark red bands at the petal bases; flowers in red, orange or brown are also possible. **'Mardi Gras'** blooms in a range of yellows, reds and bicolors on plants 18–24" tall.

Problems & Pests

Slugs, snails and fungal diseases can be problems.

Cosmos

Cosmos

Height: 1–7' **Spread:** 12–18" **Flower color:** magenta, pink, purple, white, yellow, gold, orange, red, scarlet, maroon

FEW FLOWERS, ANNUAL OR PERENNIAL, THROW SUCH A RIOTOUS party of color and form as cosmos. The most commonly grown varieties feature large, showy flowers in pink, red and white and are superb for massing at the back of the flower bed. Newer varieties bring tall, yellow blooms into the mix in addition to shorter varieties that work well as container plants. Your only disappointment will occur if you plant cosmos where it will receive less than true full sun (at least six hours, midday). These plants like their parties held on stages hot and bright.

The name cosmos is from the Greek kosmos, *meaning 'good order' or 'harmony.'*

Planting

Seeding: Indoors in late winter; direct sow after soil has warmed

Planting out: After last frost

Spacing: 12–18"

Growing

Cosmos like to grow in **full sun**. The soil should be of **poor** or **average fertility** and **well drained.** Cosmos are drought tolerant. Overfertilizing and overwatering can reduce the number of flowers produced. Yellow cosmos will do better if sowed directly in the garden.

Keep faded blooms cut to encourage more buds. Cosmos will often reseed themselves if a few flowers are left on the plants to produce the seeds.

Although these plants may need staking, they are difficult to stake. Save yourself the trouble of staking by planting cosmos in a sheltered location or against a fence, or grow shorter varieties. If staking can't be avoided, push twiggy branches into the ground when the plants are young and allow them to grow up between the branches for support. The branches will be hidden by the mature plants.

C. atrosanguineus

C. bipinnatus

Cosmos, like many warm weather annuals such as marigolds, originated in Mexico and South America.

C. sulphureus

C. *bipinnatus* (photos this page)

Tips

Cosmos are attractive in cottage gardens, at the back of a border or mass planted into an informal bed or border. Their cut flowers make lovely, long-lasting fillers in fresh arrangements.

Recommended

*C. **atrosanguineus*** (chocolate cosmos) has recently become popular among annual connoisseurs for its fragrant, deep maroon flowers that some claim smell like chocolate. The plant is upright, growing to 30" tall, but tends to flop over a bit when the stem gets too long.

*C. **bipinnatus*** (annual cosmos) has many cultivars. The flowers come in magenta, rose, pink or white, usually with yellow centers. Old varieties grow 3–6' tall while some of the newer cultivars grow 12–36" tall. **'Daydream'** has white flowers flushed with pink at the petal bases. It grows up to 5' tall. **'Psyche Mixed'** grows 3–4' tall and bears large, showy, semi-double flowers in deep lavender pink, magenta rose, white and red. **'Sea Shells'** has flowers in all colors and petals that are rolled into tubes. It grows up to 42" tall. **'Sensation'** bears large white or pink flowers and grows up to 4' tall. **Sonata Series** includes compact plants up to 24" tall that bear red, pink or white flowers.

*C. **sulphureus*** (yellow cosmos) has pale yellow, gold, orange or pale yellow-red flowers. Old varieties grow 7' tall, and new varieties grow 12"–4' tall. **'Bright Lights'** grows 3–4' tall and has semi-double, red- to orange-yellow flowers. **'Cosmic Orange'** and **'Cosmic Yellow'** are stockier plants with coarser foliage, growing 12–18" tall with orange and yellow flowers respectively. **Ladybird Series** includes compact dwarf plants, 12–14" tall, that rarely need staking. The foliage is not as feathered as in other cultivars. **'Polidor'** grows 18–24" tall and bears 2½" wide, semi-double flowers in shades of orange, yellow and red.

Problems & Pests

Cosmos rarely have any problems, but watch for wilt, aster yellows, powdery mildew and aphids.

C. bipinnatus (photos this page)

Cup Flower

Nierembergia

Height: 6–12" **Spread:** 6–12" **Flower color:** blue, purple or white, with yellow or blue centers

CUP FLOWER IS A TENDER PERENNIAL GROWN IN MUCH OF THE United States as an annual. It makes an excellent, sprawling groundcover in sun and partial shade. It resembles perennial geranium, so avoid planting the two together or the similarity might get tedious. Mix it up at the front of the border with bold-leaved perennials such as coral bells, iris and sedum.

Planting

Seeding: Indoors in mid-winter

Planting out: Spring

Spacing: 6–12"

Growing

Cup flowers grow well in **full sun** or **partial shade**. The soil should be of **average fertility, moist** and **well drained**. Fertilize little, if at all, except when growing these plants in containers.

Tips

Use cup flowers as annual groundcovers. They are also useful for bed and border edges, rock gardens, rock walls, containers and hanging baskets. These plants grow best when summers are cool, and they can withstand a light frost.

Recommended

N. **'Blue Eyes'** is a new, slightly larger-growing cultivar (at the high end of the height range). It has lacy leaves and large white flowers with blue, star-shaped eyes. It loves heat and humidity and works well as a mid-range plant in a container or as a mid-border plant.

N. caerulea (*N. hippomanica*) forms a small mound of foliage. This plant bears delicate, cup-shaped flowers in lavender blue with yellow centers. **'Mont Blanc'** is an All-America Selections winner that bears white flowers with yellow centers.

N. frutescens **'Purple Robe'** is a dense, compact plant producing deep purple flowers with golden eyes.

Problems & Pests

Slugs are likely to be the worst problem for these plants. Because cup flowers are susceptible to tobacco mosaic virus, don't plant them near any tomatoes or flowering tobaccos.

N. caerulea

Cup flowers belong to the highly poisonous nightshade family, so be sure to keep them away from children and pets.

'Mont Blanc'

Dahlberg Daisy

Golden Fleece

Thymophylla

Height: 6–12" **Spread:** 12" **Flower color:** yellow; less commonly orange

FOR BUSY GARDENERS WHO LIKE THE CLASSIC, YELLOW DAISY look but who would love to take the easy way out, I recommend Dahlberg daisies. While daisy-like annuals such as African daisy, cape marigold and cape daisy are ultimately more attractive plants, Dahlbergs will handle poor soil and overall abuse, and sometimes that's a noble thing. Their small stature also allows for varied container use, from flower boxes to mixed container plantings to hanging baskets.

Dahlberg daisy has fragrant foliage that some people compare to a lemon-thyme scent. Perhaps this is the origin of the name Thymophylla, *'thyme-leaf.'*

Planting

Seeding: Indoors in mid-winter; direct sow in spring

Planting out: After last frost

Spacing: 8–10"

Growing

Plant Dahlberg daisy in **full sun**. Any **well-drained** soil is suitable although soil of **poor** or **average fertility** is preferred. Dahlberg daisy prefers cool summers. In hot climates, it flowers in spring.

Direct-sowed plants may not flower until quite late in summer. For earlier blooms, start the seeds indoors. Don't cover the seeds, for they require light to germinate. Dahlberg daisy may self-sow and reappear each year.

Trim your plants back when flowering seems to be slowing to encourage new growth and more blooms, particularly when the weather cools.

Tips

This attractive plant can be used along the edges of borders, along the tops of rock walls or in hanging baskets or mixed containers. In any location where it can cascade over and trail down an edge, Dahlberg daisy will look wonderful.

Recommended

T. tenuiloba *(Dyssodia tenuiloba)* forms a mound of ferny foliage. From spring until the summer heat causes it to fade, it produces many bright yellow, daisy-like flowers.

This cheerful annual rarely suffers from pest or disease problems.

Dahlia

Dahlia

Height: 12"–8' **Spread:** 2–3' **Flower color:** purple, pink, white, yellow, orange, red, bicolored

BE CAREFUL AS YOU DELVE INTO THE WORLD OF DAHLIAS—SOME gardeners become so bewitched by their wide array of magnificent flowers that they plant and grow little else. Actually, becoming enchanted by dahlias is not a bad gardening bug to be bitten by, for you can spend a joyous lifetime exploring their use. Both small and large varieties look smashing as individual accent plants or in waves. Some gardeners plant beds composed solely of dahlias, creating a season-long collage of color. Smaller dahlias grown from seed are wonderful in containers while larger, tuberous specimens grow so tall and large that they can serve as annual shrubs.

Planting

Seeding: Indoors in mid- to late winter; direct sow in spring

Planting out: After last frost

Spacing: 12"

Growing

Dahlias prefer **full sun.** The soil should be **fertile,** rich in **organic matter, moist** and **well drained.** Dahlias are tuberous perennials that are treated as annuals. Tubers can be purchased and started early indoors. The tubers can also be lifted in fall and stored over winter in slightly moist peat moss. Pot them and keep them in a bright room when they start sprouting in mid- to late winter.

If there is a particular size, color or form of dahlia that you want, it is best to start it from tubers of that type. Seed-grown dahlias show a great deal of variation in color and form because the seed is generally sold in mixed packages.

To keep dahlias blooming and attractive, it is essential to remove the spent blooms.

Dahlia cultivars span a vast array of colors, sizes and flower forms, but breeders have yet to develop true blue, scented and frost-hardy varieties.

cutting bed (below)

Tips

Dahlias make attractive, colorful additions to a mixed border. The smaller varieties make good edging plants and the larger ones make good replacement plants for shrubs. Varieties with unusual or interesting flowers can be grown as attractive specimen plants.

Recommended

Of the over 20,000 dahlia hybrids, which range in height from 8" to 8', most must be grown from tubers. Tubers of specific types and colors can be purchased in late winter and early spring.

Large tuberous dahlias grow on average 3 1/2–6' tall and 2–3' wide. Truly pampered plants can reach upwards of 8' in height. Always stake tall varieties at the time of planting. Set stakes 2–2 1/2' apart. The following are on the American Dahlia Society Fabulous Fifty list. **'Inland Dynasty'** grows 4–5' tall, producing large, 14" diameter yellow, semi-cactus flowers. **'Jessie G'** forms 3 1/2" diameter, ball-type purple blooms on 5–6' plants. **'Magic Moment'** grows 4–6' tall and bears 6–8" diameter, semi-cactus, white flowers flushed lavender at the petal tips. **'Spartacus'** has intense, dark red, 8–10" diameter, informal decorative flowers on 4–5' tall plants. **'Taratahi Lilac'** grows 5' tall with 4–6" diameter, lavender-white blend, incurved cactus flowers. **'Taratahi Ruby'** produces 4–6" diameter, waterlily-type flowers on 4' tall plants. The flowers are fiery red, with a hint of orange.

Some dahlias can be started from seed with good results. Seed-started dahlias include *D.* **'Figaro,'** which forms a round, compact plant 12–16" tall. The flowers are small and double or semi-double, in a wide variety of colors. The plants grow and flower quickly and look very good grouped in a border or in containers. *D.* **'Harlequin'** forms a compact plant that flowers quickly from seed. Flowers are solid or bi-colored, single or semi-double, in many shades. Many hybrid seeds are sold in mixed packets based on flower shape, such as collarette, decorative or peony-flowered.

Problems & Pests

The most likely problems a dahlia grower may encounter are aphids, powdery mildew and slugs. If a worse problem afflicts your dahlias, it may be best to destroy the infected plants and start over.

Dahlia flowers are categorized by size, from mignons up to only 2" in diameter to giants more than 10" in diameter. They are also categorized by flower type—for example, peony, formal and informal decorative, semi-cactus and waterlily.

Informal decorative type

Semi-cactus type

Formal decorative type

Peony type

Dianthus

Sweet William

Dianthus

Height: 6–30" **Spread:** 8–12" **Flower color:** white, pink, red, purple

WITHIN THIS VERY LARGE GENUS OF PLANTS EXIST SEVERAL terrific species and varieties typically grown as biennials and annuals. Dianthus has been a favorite bedding plant for generations. These plants are excellent at or near the front of the garden bed and in all manner of containers. They tolerate air pollution, making them a good choice for small urban gardens.

Planting

Seeding: Direct sow *D. chinensis* in fall or indoors in spring; direct sow other dianthus in late spring to early summer for bloom the following year

Planting out: Spring

Spacing: 6–10"

Growing

Dianthus prefers **full sun** but tolerates some light shade. Keep these plants **sheltered** from strong winds and the hottest afternoon sun. A **light, neutral** or **alkaline, humus-rich, well-drained** soil is preferred. The most important factor in the successful cultivation of dianthus is drainage. Mix gravel into their area of the flowerbed to encourage good drainage. Growing these plants in slightly alkaline soil will produce excellent color over a long period.

D. chinensis cultivars

There are more than 300 annual and perennial species in the genus Dianthus.

D. chinensis 'Telstar Pink'

D. barbatus cultivar

Hanging baskets containing dianthus will do best if fed with liquid fertilizer twice a month. Deadhead as the flowers fade to prolong blooming. Leave a few flowers in place to go to seed, and the plants will self-seed quite easily. Seedlings may differ from the parent plants, often with new and interesting results.

Tips

Dianthus is great for mass planting and for edging flower borders and walkways. Use these plants in the rock garden, or try them as cut flowers.

Recommended

D. barbatus (sweet william) is a biennial mostly grown as an annual. It reaches a height of 18–24" and spreads 8–12". Flattened clusters of often two-toned white, pink, red or purple-red flowers bloom in late

D. barbatus cultivars with campanula and foxglove

spring to early summer. **'Hollandia Mix'** grows to 30" tall. **'Indian Summer'** is a compact plant 6–8" tall. Plants in the **Roundabout Series** grow 8–12" tall and produce solid or two-toned blooms in the first year from seed. **'Summer Beauty'** reaches a height of 12".

D. chinensis (china pink, annual pink) is an erect, mound-forming plant 6–30" tall and 8–12" wide. The fragrant flowers come in pink, red, white and light purple and are produced for an extended period in late spring and summer. Many cultivars are available. **Telstar Series** are hybrids of *D. chinensis* and *D. barbatus*, usually listed under *D. chinensis.* These plants grow 8–12" tall and wide and produce blooms in shades of pink, red and white in solid and two-toned forms.

***D.* 'Corona Cherry Magic'** grows 8–10" tall and wide and has 2½–3" wide flowers that may be solid cherry red, lavender or bicolored. This cultivar is a 2003 All-America Selections winner.

***D.* 'Rainbow Loveliness'** grows to 24" tall and bears very fragrant flowers in shades of white, pink and lavender.

Problems & Pests

Rust and *Fusarium* wilt may be problems. Providing good drainage and air circulation will keep most fungal problems away. Occasional problems with slugs and snails.

D. chinensis 'Telstar Red'

The genus name, Dianthus, *is a combination of* Dios *(a form of the name Zeus) and* anthos, *'flower,' so it means 'flower of the gods.'*

D. 'Corona Cherry Magic' with snapdragons

Diascia

Twinspur

Diascia

Height: 7–16" **Spread:** 20" **Flower color:** shades of pink, red, orange-yellow, white

LITTLE DIASCIA IS A DYNAMIC AND HEARTY BLOOMER IDEAL FOR use in containers. Its flowers are most unusual, resembling miniature bearded iris blooms or, to some, orchids. Blooms appear in late spring and carry into early fall, suspended in billowing clusters from upright, slender stems. You should start finding this relative newcomer more frequently as a transplant at local nurseries, sporting white, pink, or soft red blooms.

Planting

Seeding: Indoors in spring

Planting out: After the last frost

Spacing: 14–18"

Growing

Diascias prefer **full sun**. The soil should be **fertile, moist** and **well drained**. When hardened off, diascias withstand frost and can be planted out in early April. They generally bloom well into fall.

Many of the older diascia varieties don't thrive in high humidity and heat, but newer varieties have been bred to take the heat and still flower wonderfully throughout summer. Plants whose flowers fade during the hottest part of summer will revive and bloom again as temperatures drop in fall.

Deadheading and weekly applications of a water-soluble fertilizer will help keep blooms coming all summer. If flowering becomes sparse in searing summer heat, shear to encourage a fresh flush of blooms in a few weeks when the weather becomes cooler.

Diascias are native to the mountains of South Africa and are related to penstemons, snapdragons and foxgloves.

D. 'Little Charmer'

D. 'Coral Belle'

The genus name Diascia *comes from the Greek words* di *or* dis, *'two,' and* askos, *'sac,' referring to the two spurs each flower possesses. The alternative common name twinspur is a rough English translation of the genus name, and it is a very accurate description of the flowers.*

D. 'Strawberry Sundae'

Tips

Diascias are perennials treated as annuals. They are attractive in a rock garden or mass planted in a border. They are very nice in hanging baskets and containers when planted at the edge and allowed to cascade over and soften the side of the pot. Pinch plant tips to increase bushiness.

Recommended

D. barberae is a low-growing plant that bears loose spikes of pink flowers from mid-summer to frost. **'Blackthorn Apricot'** has apricot-colored flowers and flowerheads that point downwards. **'Pink Queen'** has light, shimmery pink flowers on long, slender stalks.

***D.* Flying Colors Series** from Proven Winners includes plants that grow 8–12" tall, are very heat and frost tolerant and have large, early-blooming flowers. **'Apricot'** has lovely apricot flowers and dense, dark green foliage. **'Coral'** has bright coral flowers. **'Trailing Antique Rose'** has a trailing habit and bears deep rose flowers.

***D.* 'Little Charmer'** grows 7–10" tall and features medium to bright pink flowers and plentiful foliage. It has excellent heat tolerance.

***D.* 'Red Ace'** is a trailing, vigorous grower reaching 10–14" in height. The abundant flowers are a very deep rose pink. It is heat tolerant.

***D.* 'Strawberry Sundae'** grows 7–10" tall with trailing stems and bright pink flowers. It does well in both the summer heat and the cooler spring and fall.

***D.* Summer Celebration Series** from Proven Selections includes great performers in the heat of summer and in the cooler spring and fall. The series boasts abundant flowers and dense, compact foliage on plants 10–16" tall. **'Coral Belle'** is a quick-growing hybrid that forms a dense mound of bright green foliage. This variety is said to be the most heat tolerant of all the diascias. The flowers are a delicate coral pink. **'Ice Pole'** bears bright white flowers that really stand out against the foliage.

D. **Whisper Series** from Simply Beautiful includes semi-trailing, spreading plants 10–15" tall. **'Cranberry Red'** has dark burgundy flowers. The series also includes **'Apricot,' 'Lavender Pink'** and **'Salmon Red,'** bearing flowers in the colors their names suggest.

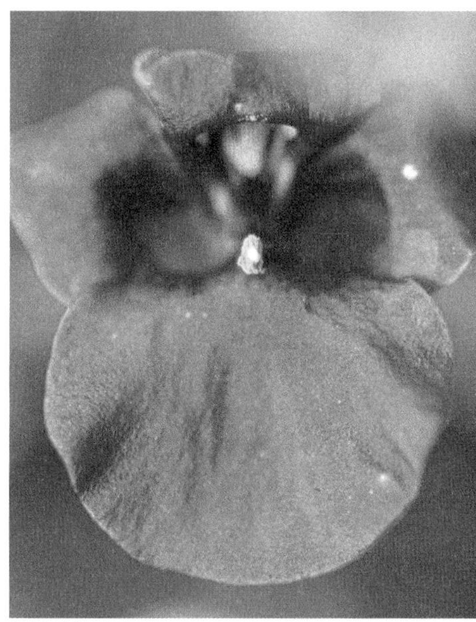

D. 'Red Ace'

In flowerbeds, diascia works especially well in cottage-style garden plantings.

Problems & Pests

Watch out for slugs.

D. 'Strawberry Sundae'

Dusty Miller

Senecio

Height: 12–24" **Spread:** equal to height or slightly narrower
Flower color: yellow or white; plant grown for silvery foliage

AS ONE ADVANCES AS A GARDENER, ONE LEARNS THAT PLANT foliage is worth as much consideration as flower size, shape and color. Dusty miller is a classic case in point. It is grown solely for its leaves. So where do you plant it? Anywhere—the plant's magnificent silver-white foliage does a wonderful job of breaking up the overpowering green of most other plants. It does indeed flower, in summer, but the blooms are not nearly as attractive as the foliage; pinch flowers off as they appear. Use dusty miller as edging (it contrasts marvelously with grass), and pop it in wherever you need to break the monotony. Don't forget to keep some handy for the edges of mixed containers, one of its chief uses.

Planting

Seeding: Indoors in mid-winter

Planting out: Spring

Spacing: 8–12"

Growing

Dusty miller prefers **full sun** but tolerates light shade. The soil should be of **average fertility** and **well drained**.

Tips

The soft, silvery, lacy leaves of this plant are its main feature, and it is used primarily as an edging plant. It is also used in beds, borders and containers. The silvery foliage makes a good backdrop to show off the brightly colored flowers of other plants.

Pinch off the flowers before they bloom. They aren't showy, and they steal energy that would otherwise go to the foliage.

'Cirrus'

Mix dusty miller with geraniums, begonias or cockscombs to really bring out the vibrant colors of those flowers.

Recommended

S. cineraria forms a mound of fuzzy, silvery gray, lobed or finely divided leaves. Many cultivars have been developed with impressive foliage colors and shapes. **'Cirrus'** has lobed, silvery green or white foliage. **'Silver Dust'** has deeply lobed, silvery white foliage. **'Silver Lace'** has delicate, silvery white foliage that glows in the moonlight.

'Cirrus' with marigolds and canna lily

Dwarf Morning Glory

Bush Morning Glory

Convolvulus

Height: 6–16" **Spread:** 10–12" **Flower color:** blue, purple, pink

HERE IS A FLOWER THAT KNOWS IT'S A FLOWER. VARIETIES OF dwarf morning glory have some of the most vividly colorful, striking blooms that you can grow in a garden. It doesn't get any prettier than 'Royal Ensign,' with its bluest of blue flowers etched by white with gold centers. I consider it the most joyous plant you can place in a flower box. All varieties feature magical, bi- and tricolored blooms. Great for the front of the bed, in baskets and anywhere the sun shines.

Planting

Seeding: Indoors in late winter; direct sow in mid- or late spring

Planting out: Mid- or late spring

Spacing: 8–10"

Growing

Dwarf morning glory prefers **full sun**. The soil should be of **poor** or **average fertility** and **well drained**. This plant may not flower well in rich, moist soil.

Soak the seeds in water overnight before planting them. If starting seeds early indoors, plant them in peat pots to avoid root damage when transplanting.

Tips

Dwarf morning glory is a compact, mounding plant that can be grown on rock walls or in borders, containers or hanging baskets.

This easy-care plant is rarely plagued by pests or diseases.

Recommended

C. ***tricolor*** bears flowers that last only a single day, blooming in the morning and twisting shut that evening. The species grows 12–16" tall. **Ensign Series** has low-growing, spreading plants that grow 6" tall. 'Royal Ensign' has deep blue flowers with white and yellow throats. **'Star of Yalta'** bears deep purple flowers whose throats pale to violet.

This annual is related to the dreaded bindweeds (Convolvulus arvensis *and* C. sepium), *but it doesn't share their unstoppable twining and spreading power.*

'White Ensign' (above), *C. tricolor* (below)

English Daisy

Bellis

Height: 2–8" **Spread:** 2–8" **Flower color:** white, pink, red; yellow centers

TEXTURED, BUTTON-SHAPED BLOOMS, ATTRACTIVE, LIGHT GREEN foliage and an upright, tidy habit make English daisies a stellar choice for both garden beds and containers. 'Habanero' is a great front-of-the-border variety, as are varieties in the Pomponette Series, with quilled petals that shimmer in bright sunlight.

Planting

Seeding: Start seed indoors in mid-winter

Planting out: In spring, when soil can be worked

Spacing: 2–6"

Growing

English daisy grows well in **full sun, partial shade** or **light shade**. The soil should be of **average to high fertility, cool, moist** and **humus rich**.

English daisy is one of the easiest plants to grow from transplants.

Tips

English daisy is a real workhorse in the garden. Use it on rock walls, in open woodland gardens, planters and borders. It can also be used as a groundcover.

English daisy has a habit of self-seeding, so it may show up where you least expect it, including in your lawn. It adapts very well in low-maintenance lawns. Deadheading to control spread is possible but decidedly time-consuming because English daisy is low growing. If immaculate lawns are required, place this plant in beds well away from lawns and consider taking the time to deadhead.

Recommended

B. perennis is a low, spreading perennial grown as an annual. Yellow-centered white, pink or red flowers bloom from mid-spring to late summer. **'Dresden China'** is a small, compact plant with light pink double flowers. **'Habanero'** has pink, white or red flowers with long petals. **Pomponette Series** has pink, red or white flowers with quilled petals. **'White Pearl'** has white double flowers.

Problems & Pests

Fungal leaf spots and aphids are possible, but not serious, problems. Watering only in the morning will prevent most problems.

Felicia

Blue Marguerite, Blue Daisy

Felicia

Height: 6–24" **Spread:** 6–24" **Flower color:** shades of blue with yellow centers

IF YOU ARE A GARDENER WHO CAN'T GET ENOUGH OF THE COLOR blue in your gardens and containers, don't overlook this irresistible charmer. Narrow petals extend like pinwheels from gold centers for a most arresting effect. This South African native is often hard to find as a transplant. If sowing seed indoors, be sure the pots or flats are kept at a cool 61° F during germination and cooler than that, if you can manage it, once seedlings emerge.

Planting

Seeding: Indoors in early spring for summer bloom; direct sow in summer for fall bloom. Stratify seeds of *F. amelloides* for three weeks before planting to boost germination.

Planting out: After last frost

Spacing: 8–12"

Growing

Felicias like **full sun**. The soil should be of **average fertility** and **well drained.** These plants do not tolerate heat well and may fade when the weather heats up.

Tips

Felicias, with their sprawling habits, are well suited to rock gardens, bed edges, mixed containers and hanging baskets. The flowers close at night and on cloudy days.

Trimming keeps plants looking their best. Pinch the tips of young plants to promote bushiness. Deadhead as the flowers fade, and cut the plants back when their flowering slows down during the heat of summer. They will revive in the cooler fall weather and produce a second flush of growth and more flowers. You can take cuttings from the new fall growth of *F. amelloides* to start plants for the following spring.

Recommended

F. amelloides forms a rounded, bushy mound 12–24" in height and spread. It bears flowers of varied shades of blue all summer. This species is a perennial grown as an annual. **'Astrid Thomas'** is a dwarf variety with medium blue flowers. It grows 10" tall with an equal spread. **'Midnight'** has deep blue flowers.

F. amelloides cultivars (photos this page)

F. bergeriana (kingfisher daisy) is a low-growing, densely hairy annual plant 6–12" tall and 6–9" wide. Yellow-centered, bright blue flowers are borne in summer.

F. heterophylla forms a low mat of grayish green foliage. It bears blue, daisy-like flowers all summer and grows 10–24" tall with an equal spread.

Problems & Pests

Felicias are generally problem free although aphids cause occasional trouble.

Flowering Flax

Linum

Height: 18–30" **Spread:** 6" **Flower color:** pink, white, red, blue, purple

HERE'S ANOTHER SUPERB ANNUAL THAT'S TOUGH TO FIND AS A transplant at the nursery. But sowing seed directly into the garden is foolproof, and the reward is a very prompt display of lovely, papery flowers in blue, white, pink, red or purple. Stems and foliage are very slender and nearly disappear from sight as plants hit full bloom, creating a delicate cloud of color. Flowering flax often blooms only from spring to the heat of midsummer, so direct sow in spring in spots that lack color the first half of the growing season.

Planting

Seeding: Direct sow in mid-spring

Planting out: Around last frost

Spacing: 4–6"

Growing

Flowering flax generally grows well in **full sun,** but during the heat of summer protect it from the hot afternoon sun. It may be better off planted in partial shade. The soil should be of **average fertility, light, humus rich** and **well drained.**

The related L. usitatissimum *is the source of the flax seeds used to produce oil and linen fiber. It has been in cultivation for more than 7000 years.*

Tips

Flowering flax can be used in borders and mixed containers and will nicely fill in the spaces between young perennials and shrubs in the landscape.

Recommended

L. grandiflorum is an upright, branching plant. It grows 18–30" tall and spreads about 6". It bears dark-centered, light pink flowers. **'Bright Eyes'** has white flowers with dark red or brown centers. It grows about 18" tall. **'Caeruleum'** bears blue or purple flowers. **'Rubrum'** flowers are deep red on plants up to 18" tall.

Problems & Pests

Excess moisture can cause stem rot and damping off. Slugs, snails and aphids can also cause problems.

Flowering Tobacco

Nicotiana

Height: 6"–5' **Spread:** 10–24" **Flower color:** red, pink, green, white, purple

FLOWERING TOBACCO IS WIDELY AVAILABLE AS A BEDDING transplant in northern nurseries, for Minnesota and Wisconsin gardeners have long appreciated the plant's many positive qualities. Plants flower from early summer to early fall. They thrive in sun but do quite well in partial shade. Newer cultivars are extremely disease resistant. Flower colors extend across a wide range (including a most unusual lime green that you'll either love or hate). I find flowering tobacco useful primarily in containers though I have seen large beds of mixed varieties that were magnificent.

Planting

Seeding: Indoors in early spring; direct sow later

Planting out: Once soil has warmed

Spacing: 6–10"

Growing

Flowering tobacco will grow equally well in **full sun** or **light** or **partial shade.** The soil should be **fertile,** high in **organic matter, moist** and **well drained.** The seeds require light for germination, so leave them uncovered.

Tips

These plants are popular in beds and borders. The dwarf varieties do well in containers.

Do not plant flowering tobacco near tomatoes because they are members of the same plant family and share many of the same diseases. Flowering tobacco may attract and harbor diseases that can kill tomatoes but will hardly affect the flowering tobacco.

Nicotiana *was named for Jean Nicot (1530–1600), a French consul in Portugal. He is credited with introducing this New World genus to France.*

N. x sanderae Nicki Series

N. sylvestris with Nicki Series

Ingesting the leaves of any *Nicotiana* species can cause severe poisoning and even death.

Recommended

***N.* Hummingbird Series** includes compact plants growing 6–12" tall and 10" wide. The fragrant flowers come in red, pink, lilac, green and white. This series is excellent at the front of a border or massed.

N. langsdorffii grows up to 3–5' tall. It bears clusters of bell-shaped, green, unscented flowers. The leaves and stems are hairy and feel sticky to the touch.

N.* x *sanderae *(N. alata* x *N. forgetiana)* is a hybrid that grows 2–5' tall and 12–16" wide. The parents are fragrant, but the hybrid and its cultivars are lightly scented to scentless. **'Avalon Bright Pink'** is a well-branched plant that grows 8–12" tall. It bears an abundance of vibrant pink flowers that contrast nicely with its dark green foliage. **Domino Series** plants are compact and grow 12–18" tall with an equal spread. Flowers come in many colors and stay open all day. **Merlin Series** has

Like sweet peas, flowering tobaccos were first cultivated for their wonderfully scented flowers. The flowers were then available only in a greenish color, and they opened only in the evening and at night. In attempts to expand the variety of colors and the daily blooming period, the scent has, in some cases, been lost.

dwarf plants ideal for mixed planters. The flowers may be red, pink, purple, white or pale green. **Nicki Series** has fragrant blooms in many colors, and the flowers stay open all day. The compact plants grow up to 18" tall. Plants in the **Sensation Series** grow up to 30" tall and bear red, white or pink flowers that stay open all day.

N. sylvestris grows up to 4' tall and 24" wide with scented white flowers. **'Only the Lonely'** can reach 4' in height and bears white blooms that are scented in the evening.

Problems & Pests

Tobacco mosaic virus, aphids, whiteflies and downy or powdery mildew may cause occasional problems.

N. sylvestris (photos this page)

Forget-Me-Not

Myosotis

Height: 6–12" **Spread:** 6" or wider **Flower color:** blue, pink, white

FORGET-ME-NOTS FEATURE TINY BLUE OR PINK FLOWERS WITH white or yellow eyes that add sparkle to partially shaded areas. I have not found it worthwhile to grow these plants in full sun, for intense summer heat quickly takes its toll. But in partial or dappled shade, their small yet bushy form and great profusion of blooms provide soothing color to the floor of a woodland garden.

Planting

Seeding: Direct sow in spring; indoors, in early spring

Planting out: Around last frost date

Spacing: 6–8"

Growing

Forget-me-not prefers **light** or **partial shade** but tolerates full sun if the weather isn't too hot. The soil should be **fertile, moist** and **well drained.** Adding lots of **organic matter** to the soil will help it retain moisture and maintain good drainage.

Seeds sown in spring will flower in mid-summer or fall. Forget-me-not will self-seed if faded plants are left in place until the following spring.

Tips

Forget-me-not can be used in the front of flowerbeds or to edge beds and borders, in mixed containers and in rock gardens and walls. You can also mix it with naturalized spring-flowering bulbs. This plant thrives in cooler parts of the garden.

Recommended

M. sylvatica forms a low mound of basal leaves. Clusters of small blue or white flowers with yellow centers are held on narrow, fuzzy stems above the foliage.

Problems & Pests

Slugs and snails, downy mildew, powdery mildew and rust may cause occasional trouble. Water in the morning to avoid pest and disease problems.

Forget-me-not is a delightful addition to woodland or wet areas and wildflower gardens.

Four-O'Clocks

Four-O'Clock Flower, Marvel of Peru

Mirabilis

Height: 18–36" **Spread:** 18–24" **Flower color:** red, pink, purple, yellow, orange, white or bicolored

FOUR-O'CLOCKS ARE SO NAMED BECAUSE THEIR PAPERY, TRUMPET-shaped flowers open mid- to late afternoon, quickly followed by the release of their lovely scent. Blooms stay open all night, making them a good choice for flower boxes on bedroom windows, where the scent will be enjoyed at bedtime. Attractive foliage and a tall, bushy habit also make four-o'clocks a fine bedding plant for the middle to rear of the border.

Planting

Seeding: Indoors in late winter; direct sow in mid-spring

Planting out: Mid-spring

Spacing: 16–24"

Growing

Four-o'clocks prefers **full sun** but tolerates partial shade. Ideally the soil should be **fertile,** but plants tolerate any **well-drained** soil.

This plant is a perennial treated as an annual, and it may be grown from tuberous roots. Dig up the tubers in fall and replant in spring. Four-o'clocks also freely self-seeds and may become weedy if allowed to renew itself in spring.

Tips

Use four-o'clocks in beds, borders, containers and window boxes. The flowers are scented, so the plant is often located near terraces or patios, where the scent can be enjoyed in the afternoon and evening.

Recommended

M. jalapa forms a bushy mound of foliage. The flowers may be solid or bicolored. A single plant may bear flowers of several colors. **'Broken Colors'** produces flowers variously marked or patterned in combinations of pink, rose, purple, orange and yellow. **'Red Glow'** bears brilliant red flowers. Plants in the **Tea Time Series** bear a single flower color on each plant. Flowers may be red, white, rose or pink.

Problems & Pests

This plant has very few problems if it is planted in well-drained soil.

Fuchsia

Fuchsia

Height: 6–36" **Spread:** 6–30" **Flower color:** pink, orange, red, purple or white; often bicolored

RAISE YOUR HAND IF YOU'VE EVER FALLEN IN LOVE WITH A magnificent hanging fuschia basket that you've spied at the nursery, taken it home and killed it. Me too. Turns out that fuchsias fry in full, mid-summer sun, regardless of your watering regimen. The trick is to hang fuchsia baskets where they will receive only half a day of sun, such as an east- or west-facing overhang, or where a tree will provide dappled, midday shade. Likewise, plant upright varieties where they receive relief from intense summer sun.

Planting

Seeding: Not recommended

Planting out: After last frost

Spacing: 12–24"

Growing

Fuchsias are grown in **partial** or **light shade.** They are generally not tolerant of summer heat, so full sun is too hot for them. The soil should be **fertile, moist** and **well drained.**

Fuchsias need to be well watered, particularly in hot weather. Ensure that the soil has good drainage because otherwise the plants can develop rot problems. Fuchsias planted in well-aerated soil with lots of perlite are almost impossible to overwater. These plants bloom on new growth, which will be stimulated by a high-nitrogen plant food.

Although fuchsias are hard to start from seed, they are easy to propagate from cuttings. Snip off 6" of new tip growth, remove the leaves from the lower third of the stem and insert

F. 'Winston Churchill'

Most fuchsias are two-toned, with one color on the inner petals and a different color on the outer petals.

F. 'Deep Purple'

F. 'Snowburner' (photos this page)

the cuttings into soft soil or perlite. Once rooted and potted, the plants will bloom all summer.

Tips

Upright fuchsias can be used in mixed planters, beds and borders. Pendulous fuchsias are most often used in hanging baskets, but these plants, with their flowers dangling from flexible branches, also make attractive additions to planters and rock gardens.

Fuchsias should be deadheaded. Pluck the swollen seedpods from behind the fading petals or the seeds will ripen and rob the plant of energy needed for flower production.

Fuchsias are perennials that are grown as annuals. To store fuchsias over winter, cut back the plants to 6" stumps after the first light frost and place them in a dark, cold but not freezing location. Water just enough to keep the soil barely moist, and do not feed. In mid-spring, repot the stumps, set them near a bright window and fertilize them lightly. Set your overwintered plants outdoors the following spring after all danger of frost has passed.

Recommended

***F.* Angels' Earrings Series** from Proven Winners includes very heat- and humidity-tolerant plants that grow 10–12" tall. **'Cascading Angel's Earrings'** has large, abundant flowers with red sepals and purple-blue petals. **'Dainty Angel's Earrings'** is a more upright plant than others in the series. The flowers have shiny red sepals and purple-blue petals. **'Snow Fire'** has a semi-trailing habit and bears bright red and white flowers.

F. x *hybrida* includes dozens of cultivars; just a few examples are given here. The upright fuchsias grow 18–36" tall, and the pendulous fuchsias grow 6–24" tall. Many available hybrids cannot be started from seed. **'Deep Purple'** has purple petals and white sepals. **'Gartenmeister Bonstedt'** is an upright, shrubby cultivar that grows about 24" tall and bears tubular, orange-red flowers. The foliage is bronzy red with purple undersides. **'Snowburner'** has white petals and pink sepals. **'Swingtime'** has white petals with pink bases and pink sepals. This plant grows 12–24" tall and spreads about 6". It can be grown in a hanging basket or as a relaxed upright plant in beds and borders. **'Winston Churchill'** has purple petals and pink sepals. The plant grows 8–30" tall, with an equal spread. It is quite upright in form but is often grown in hanging baskets.

Children, and some adults, enjoy popping the fat buds of fuchsias. The temptation to gently squeeze them is almost irresistible.

Problems & Pests

Aphids, spider mites and whiteflies are common insect pests. Diseases such as crown rot, root rot and rust can be avoided with good air circulation and drainage.

Gaura

Gaura

Height: 24"–4' **Spread:** 24–36" **Flower color:** white, pink

AS INTEREST IN TROPICAL AND TROPICAL-LOOKING GARDEN plants has grown, more nurseries are offering annual gaura, and for adventurous gardeners interested in the unusual, it is well worth seeking out. Orchid-like, pinkish white flowers up to 1" across float from narrow, branching stems from late spring through summer. Plants can reach up to four feet tall and are lovely in garden beds or very large containers.

If growing from seed, start seeds eight weeks before final frost date to ensure bloom. Gauras are not fussy about soil and do best in full sun.

Planting

Seeding: Start seed indoors in early spring

Planting out: Spring

Spacing: 18–24"

Growing

Gaura prefers **full sun** but tolerates partial shade. The soil should be **fertile, moist** and **well drained.** Gaura is drought tolerant once it is established. Most plants self-seed, and the new seedlings can be carefully transplanted if desired.

Tips

Gaura makes a wonderful addition to mixed borders. Its airy habit softens the effect of brightly colored flowers. It bears only a few flowers at a time, but if the faded flower spikes are removed, it will keep flowering all summer. Plant gaura behind low, bushy plants such as hardy geraniums, cornflowers or asters to display its delicate, floating flowers to best advantage.

Recommended

G. lindheimeri (white gaura, Lindheimer's beeblossom) is a perennial grown as an annual. It forms a large, bushy clump 3–4' tall and 24–36" wide. Spikes of small white or pinkish flowers are borne on long slender stems in summer and early fall. **'Corrie's Gold'** has a more compact habit, growing 24–36" tall. It has yellow, variegated foliage and white flowers tinged with pink. **'Siskiyou Pink'** has bright pink flowers. **'Whirling Butterflies'** is a compact, long-flowering cultivar that grows 24–36" tall. The white flowers are borne from late spring to early fall. This cultivar will not self-seed.

'Corrie's Gold'

Problems & Pests

Rare problems with rust, fungal leaf spot, downy mildew and powdery mildew can occur.

'Whirling Butterflies'

Gazania

Gazania

Height: 6–18" **Spread:** 8–12" **Flower color:** red, orange, yellow, pink, cream

GAZANIA IS THE PERFECT PLANT FOR ANY PLACE YOU'D LIKE TO throw a riotous celebration of color, for these South African natives know how to party. Few annuals feature such vibrant, multi-colored blooms, and the plant's compact habit conveniently necessitates placement near the front of the bed, where the riveting flowers will be readily seen. Long periods of high humidity do tend to take a toll, but most hot summers in the north suit gazania's cultural requirements perfectly.

Planting

Seeding: Indoors in late winter; direct sow after last frost

Planting out: After last frost

Spacing: 8–10"

Growing

Gazania grows best in **full sun** but tolerates some shade. The soil should be of **poor to average fertility, sandy** and **well drained**. This plant grows best in weather over 80° F.

Tips

Low-growing gazania makes an excellent groundcover and is also useful on exposed slopes, in mixed containers and as an edging in flowerbeds.

Recommended

G. rigens forms a low basal rosette of lobed foliage. Large, daisy-like flowers with pointed petals are borne on strong stems above the plant. The petals often have a contrasting stripe or spot. The flowers tend to close on gloomy days and in low-light situations. The species is rarely grown, but several hybrid cultivars are available. Plants of the **Daybreak Series** bear flowers in many colors, often with a contrasting stripe down the center of each petal. These flowers will stay open on dull days but close on rainy or very dark days. **Kiss Series** has compact plants with large flowers in several colors. Seeds are available by individual flower color or as a mix. **Mini-Star Series** also has compact plants. The flowers are in many colors with a contrasting dot at the base of each petal. **'Sundance'** bears flowers in reds and yellows with dark, contrasting stripes down the centers of the petals.

Problems & Pests

Overwatering is the likely cause of any problems for this plant.

Daybreak Series (above), *G. rigens* cultivar (center)

G. rigens species and cultivars (below)

Geranium

Pelargonium

Height: 8–36" **Spread:** 6"–4' **Flower color:** red, pink, orange, salmon, white, purple

THE LONGTIME POPULARITY OF GERANIUMS HAS WHIPPED PLANT breeders into a virtual non-stop frenzy of experimentation and research. The result has been many, many new varieties featuring fabulous new colors, sizes and forms. In the classic bedding geranium category, I find the Fireworks Series a must-grow—brilliant flower colors *plus* outstanding foliage. Use scented geraniums near the door and along pathways, where they can be smelled as well as seen, their heavenly scents released further by the brush of a pant leg as one passes by.

Planting

Seeding: Indoors in early winter

Planting out: After last frost

Spacing: Zonal geranium, 8–12"; ivy-leaved geranium, 24–36"; scented geraniums, 12–36"

Growing

Geraniums prefer **full sun** and tolerate partial shade, but they may not bloom as profusely. The soil should be **fertile** and **well drained**.

Geraniums grow slowly from seed, so purchasing plants may be easier. However, many species and varieties are very easy to start from seed. Start them indoors in early winter and cover with clear plastic to maintain humidity until they germinate. Once seedlings have three or four leaves, transplant them into individual 3–4" pots. Keep them in a very bright spot to maintain their compact shape.

Deadhead to keep geraniums blooming and looking neat. The flowerheads are attached to long stems that break off easily where they attach to the plant. Some gardeners prefer to snip off just the flowering end to avoid damaging the plant.

Tips

Geraniums are very popular bedding plants. Use zonal geraniums in beds, borders and containers; use ivy-leaved geraniums in hanging baskets and containers to take advantage of their trailing habit, but also as bedding plants to form a bushy, spreading groundcover; use scented geraniums in containers, especially on a deck or patio, where you can enjoy their wonderful fragrance.

P. x hortorum cultivar

The genus name Pelargonium *arises from the Greek word* pelargos, *'stork,' referring to the similarity between a stork's bill and the shape of the fruit.*

'Peppermint'

Scented cultivar (above), *P. peltatum* (below)

P. x hortorum cultivar with alyssum (below)

Geraniums are perennials that are treated as annuals. They can be kept indoors over winter in a bright room.

Recommended

P. x hortorum (bedding geranium, zonal geranium) grows up to 24" tall and 12" wide. Dwarf varieties grow up to 8" tall and 6" wide. The flowers are red, pink, purple, orange or white. **Designer Series** plants grow 12–16" tall and 10–12" wide and produce clusters of large, bright flowers in shades and combinations of red, pink, light purple, salmon and white. **Fireworks Series** is a unique new class of geranium hybrids with maple-shaped leaves and flowers that look like fireworks exploding. They are heat tolerant and great in containers. **Orbit Series** has attractive, early-blooming, compact plants. The seed is often sold in a mixed packet, but some individual colors are available. **Pillar Series** includes upright plants that grow up to 36" tall with staking. Salmon, violet and orange flowers are available. **Pinto Series** is available in all colors, and seed is generally sold by the color so you don't have to buy a mix and hope you like what you get. The flowers of **Ripple Series** are flecked and streaked with darker shades over lighter ones creating a 'ripple' effect. Plants grow 10–12" tall and wide. 'Blueberry Ripple' has light pink marked with pink-blue. 'Raspberry Ripple' bears salmon flowers marked with red.

P. peltatum (ivy-leaved geranium) grows up to 12" tall and up to 4' wide in many colors. **Cascade Series** plants are great for containers and hanging baskets. Profuse clusters of single flowers come in shades of red, pink, white, lavender and lavender-blue.

Plants in the **Summer Showers Series** can take four or more months to flower from seed. The compact plants of the **Tornado Series** are very good for hanging baskets and containers and have lilac or white flowers.

***P.* species and cultivars** (scented geraniums, scented pelargoniums) include a large number of geraniums with scented leaves. The scent categories are rose, mint, citrus, fruit, spice and pungent. In the following list, a parent of each cultivar is indicated in parentheses. Some cultivars, such as **'Apple'** *(P. odoratissimum)*, readily self-seed and stay true to form, but most must be propagated by cuttings to retain their ornamental and fragrant qualities. Many cultivars have variegated leaves. Intensely scented cultivars include **'Chocolate-Mint'** *(P. quercifolium)*, **'Lemon'** *(P. crispum)*, **'Lime'** *(P.* x *nervosum)*, **'Old-Fashioned Rose'** *(P. graveolens)*, **'Peppermint'** *(P. tomentosum)*, **'Pine'** *(P. denticulatum)*, **'Prince Rupert'** *(P. crispum)* and **'Rober's Lemon Rose'** *(P. graveolens)*.

Problems & Pests

Aphids flock to overfertilized plants but can usually be washed off before they do much damage. Leaf spot and blight may bother geraniums growing in cool, moist soil.

Edema is an unusual condition to which geraniums are susceptible. This disease occurs when a plant is overwatered. The leaf cells burst and the leaves develop a warty surface. There is no cure, but watering carefully and removing damaged leaves as the plant grows prevents the problem. The condition is more common in ivy-leaved geranium.

Fireworks Series

Ivy-leaved geranium is one of the most beautiful plants to include in a mixed hanging basket.

P. peltatum cultivars

P. x *hortorum* hybrid

Globe Amaranth

Gomphrena

Height: 6–30" **Spread:** 6–15" **Flower color:** purple, orange, magenta, pink, white, red

HERE'S AN UNUSUAL ANNUAL THAT IS TOO OFTEN OVERLOOKED by northern gardeners even though its bloom period (mid-summer to frost) brings fresh color to the garden when many perennials and annuals are feeling the strain of mid-summer heat. Globe amaranth works well in large areas, and if you are going to grow it, grow 12 or 20 in a mass, in waves or just scattered about. These flowers look delightful winding through an informal landscape or cottage garden.

Planting

Seeding: Indoors in late winter

Planting out: After last frost

Spacing: 10"

Growing

Globe amaranth prefers **full sun**. The soil should be of **average fertility** and **well drained**. This plant likes hot weather. It needs watering only when drought conditions persist.

Seeds will germinate more quickly if soaked in water for two to four days before sowing. They need warm soil, above 70° F, to sprout.

The long-lasting flowers require only occasional deadheading.

Tips

Use globe amaranth in an informal or cottage garden. This plant is often underused because it doesn't start flowering until later in summer than many other annuals. Don't overlook it—the blooms are worth the wait and provide color from the middle of summer until the first frost.

Recommended

G. globosa forms a rounded, bushy plant, 12–24" tall, that is dotted with papery, clover-like blossoms in purple, magenta, white or pink. **'Buddy'** has more compact plants, 6–12" tall, with deep purple flowers. **'Gnome Mixed'** grows 6–12" tall and has flowers in shades of white, pink and rosy purple. **'Lavender Lady'** becomes a large plant, up to 24" tall, and bears lavender purple flowers.

G. **'Strawberry Fields'** is a hybrid with bright orange-red or red flowers. It grows about 30" tall and spreads half as much.

Problems & Pests

Watch for some fungal diseases, such as gray mold and leaf spot.

The clover-like heads actually consist of showy bracts (modified leaves) from which the tiny flowers emerge.

G. globosa (photos this page)

Godetia

Clarkia, Satin Flower

Clarkia (Godetia)

Height: 8–30" **Spread:** 10–12" **Flower color:** pink, red, purple, white, some bicolored

THOUGH OFTEN DIFFICULT TO FIND AS POTTED BEDDING PLANTS, godetias are easy to direct seed. They are prized for their lovely, upright, aristocratic flowers, produced in great abundance though not for an entire season. They prefer cool summers and struggle against intense heat. Shading them from intense, early afternoon sun will greatly prolong their bloom time. Most gardeners seed in early spring, their reward a dazzling, mid-summer show. As the plants succumb to August heat, replace them with snapdragons, marigolds, petunias or salvia.

Planting

Seeding: Direct sow in spring for summer bloom or in mid- to late summer for fall bloom

Planting out: After last frost

Spacing: 6"

Growing

Godetias will grow equally well in **full sun** or **light shade**. The soil should be **well drained, light, sandy** and of **poor** or **average fertility**. Fertilizer will promote leaf growth at the expense of flower production. These plants don't like to be overwatered, so water sparingly and be sure to let them dry out between waterings. They do best in the cool weather of spring and fall.

Starting seeds indoors is not recommended. Seed plants where you want them to grow because they are difficult to transplant. Thin seedlings to about 6" apart.

Tips

Godetias are useful in beds, borders, containers and rock gardens. The flowers can be used in fresh arrangements. These plants flower quickly from seed and can be planted in early spring to provide a show of satiny flowers before the hardier summer annuals steal the show. A second planting in mid- to late summer will flower in fall.

Recommended

C. amoena (*G. amoena*, *G. grandiflora*; godetia, satin flower, farewell-to-spring) is a bushy, upright plant. It grows up to 30" tall, spreads 12" and bears clusters of ruffled, cup-shaped flowers in shades of pink, red, white and purple. **Satin Series** has compact plants that grow 8–12" tall. The single flowers come in many colors, including some bicolors.

Problems & Pests

Root rot can occur in poorly drained soil.

G. amoena (photos this page)

Heliotrope

Cherry Pie Plant

Heliotropium

Height: 8"–4' **Spread:** 12–24" **Flower color:** purple, blue, white

HELIOTROPE WAS A FAVORITE OF WELL-HEELED ENGLISH GARDENERS busy creating the great formal gardens of the Victorian era, and what they loved then, we love now. Tiny bundles of soft violet, purple, blue or white flowers are massed across upright, shrub-like plants featuring attractively veined foliage. In a garden bed, space larger varieties up to 24" apart, and grant them the same design considerations one would a trusted perennial. A single plant ('Marine' is my choice) in a properly sized pot allows the timeless beauty of heliotrope to adorn any sunny spot on your property.

Heliotrope is rarely troubled by disease, requires little maintenance and attracts butterflies with its lovely scented blooms. Try it in a patio pot or hanging basket with other sun-lovers, such as bidens or petunia.

Planting

Seeding: Indoors in mid-winter

Planting out: Once soil has warmed

Spacing: 12–24"

Growing

Heliotrope grows best in **full sun**. The soil should be **fertile,** rich in **organic matter, moist** and **well drained**. Although overwatering will kill heliotrope, the plant will also be slow to recover if left to dry to the point of wilting.

Heliotrope is sensitive to cold weather, so plant it out after all danger of frost has passed. Protect plants with newspaper or a floating row cover (available at garden centers) if an unexpected late frost or cold snap should arrive. Container-grown plants can be brought indoors at night if frost is expected.

This old-fashioned flower may have been popular in your grandmother's day. Its recent return to popularity comes as no surprise considering its attractive foliage, flowers and scent.

Plants that are a little underwatered tend to have a stronger scent.

Tips

Heliotrope is ideal for growing in containers or beds near windows and patios where the wonderful scent of the flowers can be enjoyed. 'Atlantis' and 'Nagano' are very heat-tolerant selections that do particularly well in containers and hanging baskets.

This plant can be shaped into a tree form, or standard, by pinching off the lower branches as the plant grows until it reaches the desired height and then pinching the top to encourage the plant to bush out. Create a shorter, bushier form by pinching all the tips that develop.

Heliotrope can be grown indoors as a houseplant in a sunny window. A plant may survive for years if kept outdoors all summer and indoors all winter in a cool, bright room.

Recommended

H. arborescens is a low, bushy shrub that is treated as an annual. It grows 18–24" tall, with an equal spread. Large clusters of purple, blue or white, scented flowers are produced all summer. Some new cultivars are not as strongly scented as the species. **'Atlantis'** is a heat-tolerant plant from Proven Winners that grows 10–12" tall and bears violet blue flowers. **'Blue Wonder'** is a compact plant that was developed for heavily scented flowers. Plants grow up to 16" tall with dark purple flowers. **'Dwarf Marine'** ('Mini Marine') is a compact, bushy plant with fragrant, purple flowers. It grows 8–12" tall and also makes a good houseplant for a bright location. **'Fragrant Delight'** is an older cultivar with royal purple flowers of intense fragrance. It grows 24–36" tall and may reach a height of 4' if grown as a standard. **'Marine'** has violet blue flowers and grows about 18" tall. **'Nagano,'** from Proven Winners, grows vigorously to 12–14" tall, producing deep purple flowers. **'White Delight'** is similar to 'Fragrant Delight,' but with white flowers and a stronger scent. It grows 18–24" tall.

Problems & Pests

Aphids and whiteflies can be problems for heliotrope.

In the Victorian era, heliotrope symbolized devotion and faithfulness.

Hollyhock

Alcea

Height: 5–8' **Spread:** 24" **Flower color:** yellow, cream, white, orange, pink, red, purple, reddish black

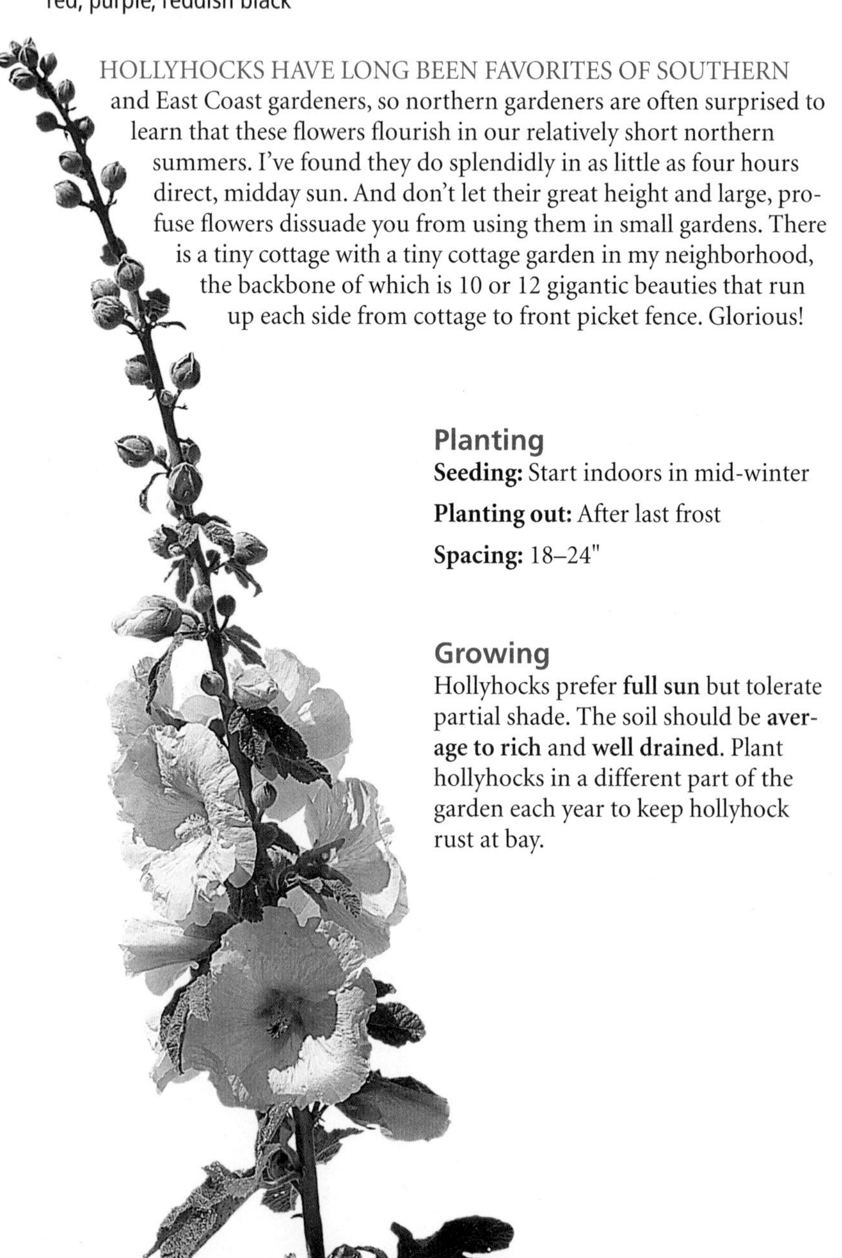

HOLLYHOCKS HAVE LONG BEEN FAVORITES OF SOUTHERN and East Coast gardeners, so northern gardeners are often surprised to learn that these flowers flourish in our relatively short northern summers. I've found they do splendidly in as little as four hours direct, midday sun. And don't let their great height and large, profuse flowers dissuade you from using them in small gardens. There is a tiny cottage with a tiny cottage garden in my neighborhood, the backbone of which is 10 or 12 gigantic beauties that run up each side from cottage to front picket fence. Glorious!

Planting

Seeding: Start indoors in mid-winter

Planting out: After last frost

Spacing: 18–24"

Growing

Hollyhocks prefer **full sun** but tolerate partial shade. The soil should be **average to rich** and **well drained.** Plant hollyhocks in a different part of the garden each year to keep hollyhock rust at bay.

Tips

Hollyhocks look best at the back of the border or in the center of an island bed. In a windy location they will need to be staked or planted against a fence or wall for support. Pinch out the main stem early in the season for shorter, bushier plants with smaller flower spikes. Shorter stems are less likely to be broken by wind and can be left unstaked.

Old-fashioned types typically have single flowers and grow much taller than newer varieties. Self-sown seedlings are often very tough, durable plants.

Recommended

A. rosea forms a rosette of basal leaves. Tall flowering stalks bear ruffled single or double blooms. **'Chater's Double'** ('Chatter's Double') bears double flowers in a wide range of colors. **'Nigra'** bears reddish black single flowers with yellow centers. **'Single Mixed'** bears carmine, pink, rose, cream or white flowers that look like hibiscus blossoms. **'Summer Carnival'** bears double flowers in yellows and reds. It blooms in early summer and produces flowers lower on the stem than other cultivars.

A. rugosa (Russian hollyhock) is similar to *A. rosea* but is more resistant to hollyhock rust. It bears pale yellow to orangy yellow single flowers.

Problems & Pests

Hollyhock rust is the biggest problem. Hollyhocks are also susceptible to bacterial and fungal leaf spot. Slugs and cutworms may attack young growth. Sometimes mallow flea beetles, aphids and Japanese beetles cause trouble.

A. rosea 'Nigra'

A. rosea *was originally grown as a food plant. The young leaves were added to salads.*

A. rosea 'Chater's Double'

Impatiens

Impatiens

Height: 6–36" **Spread:** 8–24" **Flower color:** shades of purple, red, burgundy, pink, yellow, orange, white; also bicolored and picotee

THE LIST OF SHADE-LOVING ANNUALS IS UNFORTUNATELY SHORT, but at the top of that list we are all lucky to find impatiens. What other plant brings spirited, season-long color to the dark corners of our yards and gardens? Impatiens combine effortlessly with all shade-loving perennials, making them the perfect choice for planting with hostas and ferns. They excel in containers, for you cannot overwater them. Savvy water gardeners I know grow them from a ball of soil inside an old nylon stocking wired to a hidden stake (or secured to rock), virtually floating the plants along the sides of streams and ponds.

Planting

Seeding: Indoors in mid-winter; balsam impatiens indoors in late winter. Don't cover the seeds, because they germinate best when exposed to light.

Planting out: Once soil has warmed

Spacing: 6–12"

Growing

All impatiens do best in **partial shade,** but most tolerate full shade. If kept moist, some will tolerate full sun. Of all the varieties of impatiens, Balsam and New Guinea are best adapted to sunny locations, but the latter requires afternoon shade. The soil should be **fertile, humus rich, moist** and **well drained**. New Guinea impatiens does not like wet feet, so good drainage is a must.

Tips

Busy Lizzie is known for its ability to grow and flower profusely in even deep shade. Mass plant in beds under trees, along shady fences or walls, or in porch planters. It also looks lovely in hanging baskets. The double-flowering varieties work beautifully as accent plants with hostas and in wildflower gardens.

New Guinea impatiens is almost shrubby in form and is popular in patio planters, beds and borders. This plant is grown as much for its variegated leaves as for its flowers.

Balsam impatiens, popular in the Victorian era, is experiencing a resurgence in popularity. Its habit is more upright than that of most other impatiens, and it is attractive when grouped in beds and borders.

I. balsamina

The botanical name for impatiens was once Sultani, *after the Sultan of Zanzibar, from whose cool, moist lands this plant originated.*

I. hawkeri cultivar

I. walleriana cultivar (above), *I. hawkeri* cultivar (below)

Recommended

New impatiens varieties are introduced every year, expanding the selection of size, form and color.

I. balsamina (balsam impatiens) grows 12–36" tall and up to 18" wide. The flowers come in shades of purple, red, pink or white. There are several double-flowered cultivars, such as **'Camellia-flowered,'** with pink, red or white flowers on plants up to 24" tall; **'Tom Thumb,'** with pink, red, purple or white flowers on compact plants to 12" tall; and **'Topknot,'** with large flowers in a similar range of colors held above the foliage on plants 12" tall.

***I. hawkeri* New Guinea Hybrids** (New Guinea impatiens) grow 12–30" tall and 12" wide or wider. The flowers come in shades of red, orange, pink, purple or white. The foliage is often variegated with a yellow stripe down the center of each leaf. **Firelake Series** grows 12–18" tall, bearing large flowers in a range of colors. The foliage is variegated dark red, green, white or cream. **Java Series** are compact, well-branched plants 10–14" tall. Abundant flowers bloom in shades of red, rose, orange, salmon, pink, violet and white. The foliage ranges from green to bronze. **'Tango'** grows 12–14" tall. It has dark bronze-green foliage and deep orange flowers that bloom from summer to fall.

***I.* Seashell Series** is a group of new African hybrids with flowers in shades of yellow, orange, apricot and pink. Plants grow 8–10" tall and spread about 12".

I. walleriana (busy Lizzie) grows 6–18" tall and up to 24" wide. The flowers come in shades of red, orange, pink, purple or white, or are bicolored. **Dazzler Series** are abundantly colorful, floriferous plants 10–14" tall and 8–10" wide. **Fiesta Series** grows about 12" tall and wide and bears double flowers in shades of pink, orange, red and burgundy. They almost resemble small rose bushes. **Mosaic Series** plants have uniquely colored flowers, with the margins and most of the petals speckled in a darker shade of the petal color. **Super Elfin Series** are commonly available cultivars that come in many shades, including bicolors. The compact plants grow about 12" tall, but they may spread more. **Tempo Series** grows 10–14" tall and has flowers in 27 different colors. **'Victorian Rose'** is an All-America Selections winner with deep pink, double or semi-double flowers.

Problems & Pests

Fungal leaf spot, stem rot, thrips, *Verticillium* wilt, whiteflies and aphids can cause trouble.

I. walleriana cultivars (photos this page)

With their reliable blooming in shade, and their wide variety of colors and types, impatiens are one of America's top-selling bedding plants.

Lantana

Shrub Verbena

Lantana

Height: 6–42" **Spread:** 12–42" **Flower color:** yellow, orange, pink, purple, red, white; often in combination

WHEN IT'S TIME TO POT THE 40 OR SO CONTAINERS THAT WILL ultimately be scattered across the steps, stoops, patio and pathways encompassing my humble half-acre, the first thing I load up on is lantana. 'Spreading Sunset,' or like varieties featuring clusters of tiny orange and red flowers, combine magically in pots with blue varieties of salvia, ageratum, browallia and lobelia.

Planting

Seeding: Not recommended

Planting out: Into warm soil after danger of frost has passed

Spacing: 12–42"

Growing

Lantanas grow best in **full sun** but tolerate partial shade. They prefer soil that is **fertile, moist** and **well drained** but can handle heat and drought. Take cuttings in late summer if you would like plants for the following summer but don't want to store a large one over winter.

Tips

Lantanas are tender shrubs grown as annuals. They are useful in beds, borders, mixed containers and hanging baskets. These plants can handle heat, making them perfect for low-maintenance gardens.

Recommended

L. camara is a bushy plant bearing round clusters of flowers in many colors. **Lucky Series** plants grow 10–14" tall and have a neat upright habit. They do well in the heat and with restricted water. **'New Gold'** grows 24" tall and bears clusters of bright yellow flowers. **'Spreading Sunset'** bears brightly colored orange to red flowers.

L. montevidensis **'Weeping Lavender'** grows 6–12" tall. Its slender stems trail to 36" long and bear dense clusters of pinkish lilac flowers.

L. **Patriot Series** plants flower in a wide range of colors and have minty, dark to mid-green foliage. **'Dove Wings'** grows 24" tall and 12" wide with pure white flowers. **'Hallelujah'** grows 42" tall and wide. Flowers

'Spreading Sunset' (photos this page)

change from yellow-gold to orange-pink and finally lavender. **'Hot Country'** grows 36" tall and wide and produces sienna yellow blooms that mature quickly to fuchsia. **'Rainbow'** is a compact plant growing 12" tall and wide with large, dark green leaves and yellow, orange and pink flowers.

Problems & Pests

Lantana is subject to infestations of whiteflies.

Larkspur

Rocket Larkspur, Annual Delphinium

Consolida

Height: 12"–4' **Spread:** 6–14" **Flower color:** blue, purple, pink, gray, white; sometimes bicolored

LARKSPUR IS AN EXCELLENT CHOICE FOR THE BACK OF THE GARDEN, delivering a strong vertical accent in sun to partial shade. One of the tallest annuals, the plant carries its profuse spires of flowers with an airy nonchalance that fits perfectly with the casual tones of cottage gardens and large, informal plantings. Combine tall, purple, blue and white varieties with pink and red cosmos of equal height for a riot of towering color. Newer dwarf varieties such as those found in the Dwarf Rocket Series are wonderful additions to the world of container gardening. All varieties are great for cutting.

Planting

Seeding: Indoors in mid-winter; direct sow in early or mid-spring, as soon as soil can be worked

Planting out: Mid-spring

Spacing: 6–12"

Growing

Larkspur does equally well in **full sun** or **light shade**. The soil should be **fertile**, rich in **organic matter** and **well drained**. Keep the roots cool and add a light mulch; dried grass clippings or shredded leaves work well. Don't put mulch too close to the base of the plant or crown rot may develop.

Plant seeds in peat pots to prevent root damage when the seedlings are transplanted. Seeds started indoors may benefit from being chilled in the refrigerator for one week prior to sowing.

Deadhead to keep larkspur blooming well into fall.

Tips

Plant groups of larkspur in mixed borders or cottage gardens. The tallest varieties may require staking.

Recommended

C. ambigua (*C. ajacis*) is an upright plant with feathery foliage. It bears spikes of purple, blue, pink or white flowers. **Dwarf Rocket Series** includes plants that grow 12–20" tall and 6–10" wide and bloom in many colors. **'Earl Grey'** grows 3–4' tall, bearing flowers in an intriguing color between slate and gunmetal gray. **'Frosted Skies'** grows to 18" tall and bears large, semi-double flowers in a beautiful bicolor of blue and white. Plants in the **Giant Imperial Series** flower in many colors and grow 24–36" tall and up to 14" wide. **Sydney Series** plants grow 4' tall and 10–14" wide. They bear spikes of long-lasting double flowers 1 1/2" across, in purple, rose or white.

C. ambigua (photos this page)

Problems & Pests

Slugs and snails are potential troublemakers. Powdery mildew and crown or root rot are avoidable if you water thoroughly, but not too often, and make sure the plants have good air circulation.

Lavatera

Annual Mallow

Lavatera

Height: 18"–10' **Spread:** 18"–5' **Flower color:** pink, salmon, white, red, purple

LAVATERA HAS BECOME INCREASINGLY AVAILABLE IN NURSERIES, and small wonder. These are large, bushy annuals with lovely, often richly veined, open flowers and attractive, maple leaf-shaped foliage. *L. trimestris* is superb in the middle to rear of the garden bed while the taller varieties serve as long-blooming annual shrubs.

Planting

Seeding: Direct sow in spring, or start indoors in late winter

Planting out: After last frost

Spacing: 18–24"

Growing

Lavatera prefers **full sun** but may appreciate some shade from the hot afternoon sun. It performs best in cool, moist weather. The soil should be of **average fertility, light** and **well drained.**

This plant resents having its roots disturbed and tends to do better when direct sown. If you start seeds indoors, use peat pots or peat pellets to avoid disturbing the roots when transplanting.

Tips

Lavatera can be used as a colorful backdrop behind smaller plants in a bed or border. Very tall varieties can be used as temporary hedges along property lines, driveways and patios. The blooms make attractive cut flowers and are edible.

L. trimestris 'Silver Cup' with verbena

Lavatera is often called annual mallow, and it is in the same family as the true mallows (genus Malva*).*

L. trimestris

L. t. 'Mont Blanc' (above), *L. t.* 'Silver Cup' (below)

Lavatera grows to be fairly large and shrubby, so stake tall varieties to keep them from falling over in summer rain showers.

Recommended

L. arborea (tree mallow) is a large plant, capable of growing 10' tall and spreading 5'. The funnel-shaped flowers are pinkish purple. The lifespan of this plant is undetermined. Typically grown as an annual, it can sometimes be treated as a biennial or perennial. The cultivar **'Variegata'** has cream-mottled leaves.

L. cachemiriana has light pink flowers. It can grow up to 8' tall and is usually half as wide. It is native to Kashmir.

L. trimestris is a bushy plant up to 4' tall and 18–24" wide. It bears red, pink or white funnel-shaped flowers. **Beauty Series** includes 'Pink Beauty,' which grows 24" tall with light pink flowers; 'Rose Beauty,'

which grows 24–30" tall with rose pink flowers; 'Salmon Beauty,' which grows 24–30" tall with salmon pink flowers; and 'White Beauty,' which grows 18–24" tall with white flowers. **'Mont Blanc'** bears white flowers on compact plants that grow to about 20" tall. **'Silver Cup'** grows 24–30" tall and has large, cup-shaped, light pink flowers with dark pink veins.

Problems & Pests

Plant lavatera in well-drained soil to avoid root rot. Destroy any rust-infected plants. This plant may attract Japanese beetles.

'Mont Blanc' (above), 'Silver Cup' with verbena and cleome (below)

Lisianthus

Prairie Gentian

Eustoma

Height: 8–36" **Spread:** usually half the height **Flower color:** blue, purple, pink, yellow, white

FLORISTS HAVE LONG PRIZED THE CURLED, ROSE-LIKE BLOOMS OF lisianthus, and many gardeners are now growing this lovely annual for use as a cut flower. It makes a wonderful bedding plant and combines well with sunflower, coreopsis and annuals with daisy-like flowers. 'Forever Blue' is readily found as a transplant at nurseries. For the cutting garden, plants in the Echo Series are worth seeking out or growing from seed.

Planting

Seeding: Indoors in early winter

Planting out: Mid-spring

Spacing: 4–12"

Growing

Lisianthus prefers **full sun** but in hot weather benefits from light or partial shade to protect it from the afternoon sun. The soil should be of

average fertility and **well drained**. A **neutral** or **alkaline pH** is preferred.

Seedlings can be quite slow to establish when seeds are sown directly. It is best to either start lisianthus very early indoors with good light or purchase it at the garden center.

Tips

All varieties of lisianthus look best grouped in flowerbeds or containers. The tallest varieties, with their long-lasting blooms, are popular in cut-flower gardens.

Recommended

E. grandiflorum forms a slender, upright plant 24–36" tall topped by satiny, cup-shaped flowers. **Echo Series** is popular, with flowers in many colors. The plants are tall, to about 24", and are admired for their double flowers, which are perfect for fresh arrangements. **'Forever Blue'** is a compact plant that grows only 10–14" tall. This All-America Selections winner has blue, tulip-like flowers. **Heidi Hybrids Mix** plants grow 18–20" tall and 8–10" wide. They have sturdy, branched stems bearing single flowers in shades of blue, pink, lilac, white and yellow. **Lisa Series**, a popular dwarf variety, blooms in many colors and grows to about 8" tall; it is reputed to bloom from seed one month sooner than other varieties.

Problems & Pests

Generally, lisianthus is trouble free; however, several diseases, including *Fusarium* wilt, can kill it. Purchase treated seed from a reputable source, and destroy any plant that appears diseased before the diseases have a chance to spread.

A small vase filled with satin-textured lisianthus flowers will add a touch of elegance to any table.

Lobelia
Edging Lobelia
Lobelia

Height: 3–10" **Spread:** equal to or twice the height **Flower color:** purple, blue, pink, white

LOBELIAS ARE WONDERFUL AS CUT FLOWERS. THEIR LIGHT, graceful form and feathery blooms are a flower arranger's delight. They also do well in rock gardens, around stone walls and near other stone features, where their fragile appearance contrasts splendidly with the brutish look of stone. Lobelias bloom from late spring to fall, making the trailing varieties extremely useful in hanging baskets and window boxes.

Planting

Seeding: Indoors in mid-winter

Planting out: After last frost

Spacing: 6"

Growing

Lobelia grows well in **full sun** or **partial shade.** The soil should be **fertile,** high in **organic matter, moist** and **well drained.** Lobelia likes cool summer nights. In hot weather, make sure that its soil stays moist.

Lobelia seedlings are susceptible to damping-off. See the 'Starting Annuals from Seed' section (p. 29–32) for information on proper propagation techniques to help prevent damping-off.

Tips

Use lobelia along the edges of beds and borders, on rock walls, in rock gardens, in mixed containers or in hanging baskets.

Trim lobelia back after the first wave of flowers. It stops blooming in the hottest part of summer but usually revives in fall.

Recommended

L. erinus may be rounded and bushy or low and trailing. It bears blue to violet flowers with yellow to white throats. **'Big Blue'** flowers well through the season. **Cascade Series** plants have a trailing form and flowers in many shades. **'Crystal Palace'** rarely grows over 4" tall and has dark green foliage and dark blue flowers. **'Laguna Compact Blue with Eye'** is the most heat-tolerant variety to date. It grows to 10" tall and produces sky blue flowers. **'Laguna Pink'** is a trailing, heat-tolerant plant with dusky pink flowers. It grows to 6" tall and 14" wide. Cultivars in the **Regatta Series** are trailing, tolerate heat well and bloom longer than many other cultivars. **Riviera Series** plants are bushy, grow only 3–4" tall and have blue and purple flowers. **'Sapphire'** has white-centered blue flowers on trailing plants.

'Sapphire'

Problems & Pests

Rust, leaf spot and slugs may be troublesome.

Cascade Series

Love-in-a-Mist

Nigella

Height: 16–24" **Spread:** 8–12" **Flower color:** blue, white, pink, purple

LOVE-IN-A-MIST IS APTLY NAMED, FOR THE WISPY, THREAD-LIKE foliage does indeed create the effect of flower blooms floating in a greenish mist. This is an excellent annual for large areas, and it looks wonderful planted in waves on a hillside. The plant is not often found as a nursery transplant, but it is easy to grow from seed—just scatter seed on tilled soil and rake lightly until the seed is barely covered. If you'd like it in the same area year after year, refrain from deadheading, and it will reseed itself. Do deadhead, though, to keep new flowers coming. The seedheads that form after flowering are quite attractive and prized for use in dried-flower arrangements.

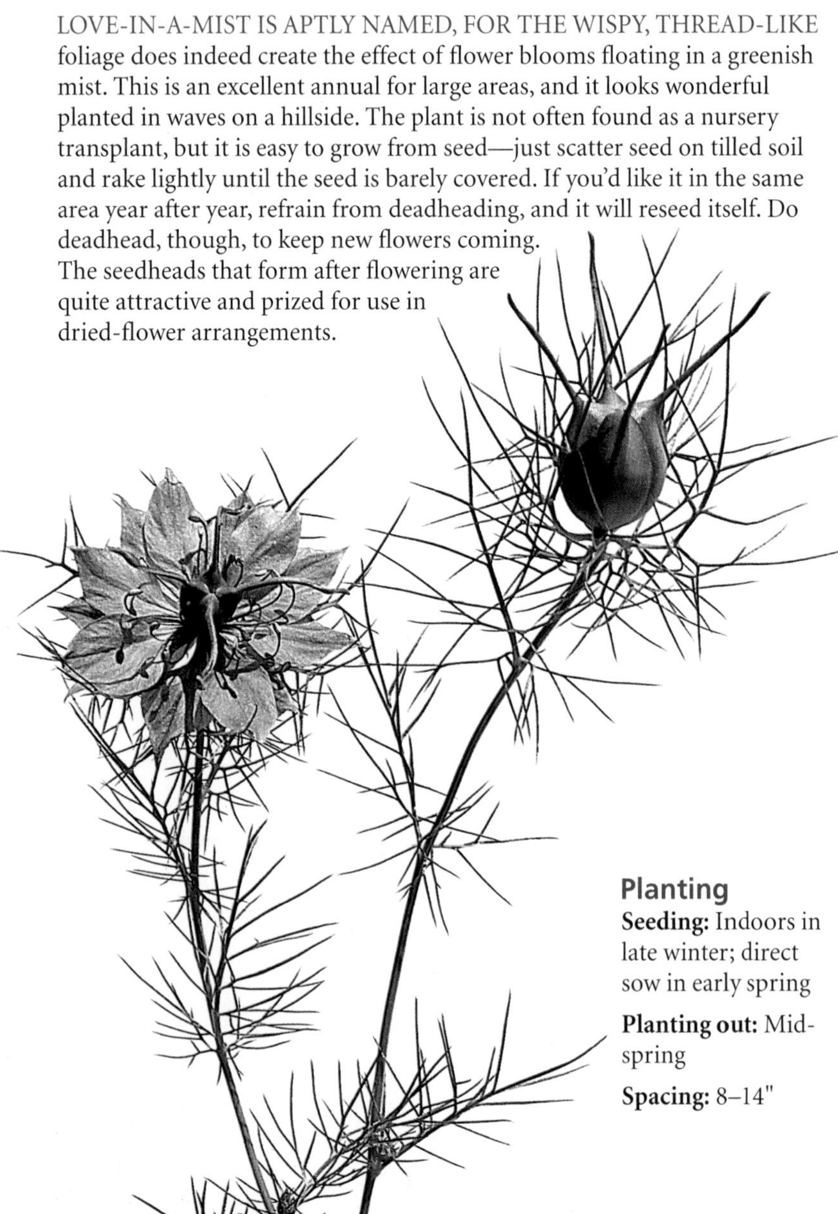

Planting

Seeding: Indoors in late winter; direct sow in early spring

Planting out: Mid-spring

Spacing: 8–14"

Growing

Love-in-a-mist prefers **full sun**. The soil should be of **average fertility, light** and **well drained**.

Direct sow seeds every two weeks all spring to prolong the bloom. This plant resents having its roots disturbed. Start seeds indoors in peat pots or pellets to avoid damaging the roots when transplanting.

Tips

This attractive, airy plant is often used in mixed beds and borders. The blooming may slow down and the plants may die back if the weather gets too hot during summer.

The stems of this plant can be a bit floppy and may benefit from being staked with twiggy branches. Poke the branches in around the plants while they are young, and the plants will grow up between the twigs.

Recommended

N. damascena forms a loose mound of finely divided foliage. It grows 18–24" tall and spreads about half this much. The light blue flowers darken as they mature. Plants in the **Miss Jekyll Series** grow to about 18" and bear semi-double flowers in rose pink, sky blue or a deep cornflower blue that pairs especially well with the golden yellow of coreopsis. **'Mulberry Rose'** bears light pink flowers that mature to dark pink. **Persian Jewels Series** contains some of the most common cultivars, with plants that grow to about 16" tall and have flowers in purple, rose and white.

N. damascena (photos this page)

Love-in-a-mist has a tendency to self-sow and may show up in unexpected spots in your garden for years to come.

Madagascar Periwinkle

Vinca Rosea

Catharanthus

Height: 10–24" **Spread:** equal to or greater than height **Flower color:** red, pink, apricot or white, often with contrasting centers

MADAGASCAR PERIWINKLE IS PERHAPS THE PERFECT BEDDING plant. It blooms for a great length of the northern growing season, loves hot, humid summers, comes in a variety of flower colors and heights and sports dark green, oval foliage that perfectly sets off the rounded petals that make up each flower. New varieties appear nearly every year, such that you'll find a good selection of colors to choose from at your local nursery.

Planting

Seeding: Indoors in mid-winter

Planting out: After last frost and when the soil has warmed

Spacing: 8–18"

Growing

Madagascar periwinkle prefers **full sun** but tolerates partial shade. Any **well-drained** soil is fine. This plant tolerates pollution and drought, but it prefers to be watered regularly. It doesn't like to be too wet or too cold.

Keep seedlings warm and take care not to overwater them. The soil temperature should be 55°–64° F for seeds to germinate.

Tips

Plant Madagascar periwinkle in a bed along an exposed driveway or against the south-facing wall of the house because this plant enjoys the heat. It can also be used in hanging baskets, in planters and as a temporary groundcover.

Recommended

C. roseus is a perennial grown as an annual. It forms a 12–24" mound of strong stems. The flowers are pink, red or white, often with contrasting centers. **'Apricot Delight'** is a 10–12" plant that bears pale apricot flowers with bright raspberry red centers. **Cooler Series** plants are 10–14" tall. They bear light-colored flowers with darker, contrasting centers. All-America Selections winner **'Jaio Dark Red'** is a 10–15" plant that has large (2 1/2" wide), very red flowers with a small white eye. **'Jaio Scarlet Eye,'** another All-America Selections winner, produces a profusion of plants that grow 12" tall and have flowers in various colors.

Problems & Pests

Slugs can be troublesome. Most rot and other fungal problems can be avoided by not overwatering.

'Jaio Scarlet Eye'

In a bright room, Madagascar periwinkle can be grown as a houseplant.

C. roseus cultivar

Marigold

Tagetes

Height: 7–36" **Spread:** 12–24" **Flower color:** yellow, red, orange, gold, cream, bicolored

MARIGOLDS HAVE DECLINED IN USE AS HIPPER, MORE ENTICING annuals have made the nursery scene, but plant hybridizers continue to experiment with this old-fashioned stalwart, with pleasing results. Today a huge number of marigolds are available, many offering far different flower styles from the stuffy cushion form that grandma grew. The color palette has also increased greatly and includes many new bicolored varieties. One thing has remained constant: marigolds are easy to grow, withstand heat and tolerate dry conditions. They are certainly worth a fresh look.

When using marigolds as cut flowers, remove the lower leaves to take away some of the pungent scent.

Planting

Seeding: Start indoors in spring or earlier

Planting out: Once soil has warmed

Spacing: Dwarf marigolds, 6"; tall marigolds, 12"

Growing

Marigolds grow best in **full sun**. The soil should be of **average fertility** and **well drained**. These plants are drought tolerant and hold up well in windy, rainy weather.

Remove spent blooms to encourage more flowers and to keep plants tidy.

Tips

Mass planted or mixed with other plants, marigolds make a vibrant addition to beds, borders and container gardens. These plants will thrive in the hottest, driest parts of your garden.

Recommended

T. erecta (African marigold, American marigold, Aztec marigold) is 20–36" tall, with huge yellow to orange flowers. **Cracker Jack Series** plants reach up to 36" in height and bear large double flowers in bright

T. erecta

T. erecta *and* T. patula *are often used in vegetable gardens for their reputed insect-repelling qualities.*

T. patula cultivar

T. tenuifolia

T. tenuifolia (above), T. patula cultivar (below)

shades of orange and yellow. **'Inca'** bears double flowers in solid or multi-colored shades of yellow, gold and orange on compact plants that grow to 18" tall. **'Marvel'** is another compact cultivar, growing only 18" tall but with the large flowers that make the species popular. **'Vanilla'** bears unique, cream white flowers on compact, odorless plants.

T. patula (French marigold) is low growing, only 7–10" tall. **Bonanza Series** includes popular double-flowered cultivars. The flowers are red, orange, yellow or bicolored. **Hero Series** plants grow only 8–10" tall and bear double flowers, with some bicolors. **Janie Series** includes popular early-blooming, compact plants with red, orange or yellow double blooms. **'Jolly Jester'** is a bushy plant growing to 24" tall, producing bright orange and red striped, single flowers. **'Naughty Marietta'** grows 12–14" tall and bears large, single gold flowers with a maroon blotch on each petal. **Safari Series** plants grow 12" tall and have $2^1/_2$" wide, double flowers.

T. tenuifolia (signet marigold) has dainty single flowers that grow on bushy plants with lacy foliage. **Gem Series** plants are commonly available. The compact plants, about 10" tall, bear flowers in shades of yellow and orange, and the edible blooms last all summer. **'Starfire'** bears single flowers in shades of yellow, orange and red, all with a band of dark red near the base of each petal.

***T.* Triploid Hybrids** (triploid marigold) have been developed by crossing *T. erecta* and *T. patula*. The resulting plants have the huge flowers of African marigold and the compact growth of French marigold. These hybrids are the most heat resistant of all the marigolds. They generally grow about 12" tall and spread 12–24". **'Nugget'** bears large yellow, red, orange, gold or bicolored flowers on low, wide-spreading plants. **'Trinity Mixed'** are compact plants that grow to 12" tall. Large 3" wide flowers come in solid and mixed shades of oranges, yellows and mahogany red. Plants in the **Zenith Series** have semi-double to double flowers in many yellow, orange or red shades or bicolors.

Problems & Pests

Slugs and snails can chew marigold seedlings to the ground. Thrips and mites may develop in mature foliage.

'Jolly Jester'

T. tenuifolia *is used as a culinary or tea herb in some Latin American countries, where it is native.*

T. erecta

Mexican Sunflower

Tithonia

Height: 24"–6' **Spread:** 12–24" **Flower color:** orange, red-orange, yellow

FEW PLANTS SO READILY CONJURE UP VISIONS OF THEIR NATIVE land as Mexican sunflowers. Witness their thick stems, large leaves and festive, orange or yellow flowers, and one senses the plant comes from an arid land far south of our states' borders. Mexican sunflowers are an enjoyable oddity, some varieties easily surpassing five feet in height. Like sunflowers, these plants are a wonderful first seed-planting experience for children. Most useful to serious gardeners is the All-America Selections winner 'Fiesta del Sol,' its compact form making it handy for creating splashes of color in large, informal beds.

Planting

Seeding: Indoors in early spring; direct sow in spring

Planting out: Once soil has warmed

Spacing: 10–20"

Growing

Mexican sunflower grows best in **full sun**. The soil should be of **average to poor fertility** and **well drained**. Cover seeds lightly; they germinate better when exposed to some light. Mexican sunflower needs little water or care but blooms more profusely if deadheaded regularly.

Tips

Mexican sunflower is heat resistant, so it is ideal for growing in a sunny, dry, warm spot such as under the eaves of a south-facing wall. The plants are tall and break easily if exposed to too much wind. Grow them along a wall or fence to provide shelter and stability. This coarse annual is well suited to the back of a border, where it will provide a good backdrop to a bed of shorter plants.

Recommended

T. rotundifolia is a vigorous, bushy plant. It grows 36"–6' tall and spreads 12–24". Vibrant orange-red flowers are produced from mid- to late summer through to frost. The leaves and stems are covered in a downy fuzz. **'Fiesta del Sol'** bears bright orange flowers on plants about 30" tall. **'Goldfinger'** grows 24–36" tall and bears large orange flowers. **'Torch'** flowers are a vivid red-orange. **'Yellow Torch'** has bright yellow flowers.

Problems & Pests

This plant is generally resistant to problems; however, young foliage may suffer slug and snail damage. Aphids can become a problem if not dealt with immediately.

T. rotundifolia

For a hot look along a sunny fence or wall, mix Mexican sunflower with other sunflowers and marigolds.

'Torch'

Monkey Flower

Mimulus

Height: 6–12" **Spread:** 12–24" **Flower color:** orange, yellow, pink, red, cream or bicolors

MONKEY FLOWER IS AN EXCEPTIONAL BEDDING PLANT, AND ONE of the few annuals available to northern gardeners that will perform well in partial shade and naturally wet soils. I've seen it edging ponds and bog gardens in addition to enlivening flower boxes and containers in half-day sun or dappled shade. So named because the blooms resemble the face of a smiling monkey (sort of), the plant's attractive, dense foliage looks good as a groundcover in moist areas.

Planting

Seeding: Indoors in early spring

Planting out: Once soil warms after last frost

Spacing: 10–12"

Growing

Monkey flowers prefer **partial** or **light shade**. Protection from the afternoon sun will prolong the blooming of these plants. The soil should be **fertile, moist** and **humus rich**. Don't allow the soil to dry out. These plants can become scraggly and unattractive in hot sun.

Tips

Monkey flowers make an excellent addition to a border near a pond or to a bog garden. In a flowerbed, border or container garden, they will need to be watered regularly.

These plants are perennials that are grown as annuals. They can be kept over the winter indoors in a cool, bright room.

Recommended

M.* x *hybridus is a group of upright plants with spotted flowers. They grow 6–12" tall and spread 12". **'Calypso'** bears flowers in orange, yellow, red and pink. **'Mystic Mixed'** is compact and early flowering in bright red, yellow, pink, orange and cream colors in solids or bicolors.

M. luteus (yellow monkey flower), though not as common as the hybrids, is worth growing for its spreading habit and attractive yellow flowers. It grows about 12" tall and spreads up to 24". The yellow flowers are sometimes spotted with red or purple.

Problems & Pests

Downy or powdery mildew, gray mold, whiteflies, spider mites and aphids can cause problems.

'Mystic Mixed'

These plants tend to fade in summer heat, so they work well in damp, partly shaded spots.

M. luteus

Morning Glory

Moonflower, Sweet Potato Vine, Mina Lobata

Ipomoea

Height: 15"–15' **Spread:** 12"–15' **Flower color:** white, blue, pink, red, yellow, orange, purple, sometimes bicolored; some types grown for foliage

ONE OF THE MOST BEAUTIFUL OF ALL VINING/CLIMBING PLANTS, morning glory has maintained its popularity for centuries. Large, circular blooms in a wide range of colors are offset by handsome, heart-shaped leaves. For something different, plant morning glories along the edge of evergreen trees or shrubs, then allow the plants to climb the tree—look, my arborvitae is in bloom! Trailing varieties of sweet potato vine, with their compelling purple or lime green leaves, are outstanding in hanging baskets, window boxes and large containers.

Planting

Seeding: Indoors in early spring; direct sow after last frost

Planting out: Late spring

Spacing: 12–18"

Growing

Grow these plants in **full sun**. Any type of soil will do, but a **light, well-drained** soil of **poor to average fertility** is preferred. *I. alba* needs warm weather to bloom.

These plants must twine around objects in order to climb them. Wide fence posts, walls or other broad objects must have a trellis or some wire or twine attached to provide the vines something to grow on.

To speed germination, nick the seed's hard coat prior to soaking. Soak seeds for 24 hours before sowing. If starting seeds indoors, plant them in individual peat pots.

Tips

These vines can be grown anywhere: fences, walls, trees, trellises and arbors are all possible supports. As groundcovers, morning glories will grow over any obstacles they encounter. They can also be grown in hanging baskets.

If you have a bright sunny window, consider starting a hanging basket of morning glories indoors for a unique winter display. The vines will twine around the hangers and spill over the sides of the pot, providing you with beautiful trumpet flowers, regardless of the weather outside.

Each flower of a morning glory plant lasts only one day. The buds form a spiral that slowly unfurls as the day brightens with the rising sun.

I. alba

Grow moonflower on a trellis near a porch or patio that is used in the evenings, so that the sweetly scented flowers can be fully enjoyed. Once evening falls, the huge, white blossoms pour forth their sweet nectar, attracting night-flying moths.

I. tricolor

I. batatas 'Tricolor' (above), *I. batatas* 'Blackie' (below)

Recommended

I. alba (moonflower) has sweet-scented, white flowers that open only at night. It grows up to 15' tall.

I. batatas (sweet potato vine) is a twining climber that is grown for its attractive foliage rather than its flowers. Often used in planters and hanging baskets, sweet potato vine can be used by itself or mixed with other plants. It may spread or climb 10' or more in a summer. As a bonus, when you pull up your plant at the end of summer, you can eat the enlarged tuber-like roots (sweet potatoes). **'Black Heart'** is more compact than the species. It has heart-shaped, dark purple-green foliage with darker veins. **'Blackie'** has dark purple (almost black), deeply lobed leaves. **'Margarita'** has yellow-green foliage and fairly compact growth. This cascading plant can also be trained to grow up a trellis. **'Tricolor'** has foliage variegated pink, green and white. It is not as vigorous as the others, growing to only 15".

I. lobata (mina lobata, firecracker vine, exotic love) is a twining climber 6–15' tall. The flowers are borne along one side of a spike. The buds are red and the flowers mature to orange then yellow, giving the spike a fire-like appearance.

I. purpurea (common morning glory) is a twining climber that grows 6–10' tall. It bears trumpet-shaped flowers in purple, blue, pink or white. **'Grandpa Ott'** bears pinky purple flowers with darker purple stripes. **'Knowilan's Black'** bears dark purple flowers.

I. tricolor (morning glory) is a twining climber that can grow 10–12' tall in a single summer. There are many cultivars of this species available, but some listed as such may actually be cultivars of *I. nil.* **'Blue Star'** bears blue and white streaked flowers. **'Heavenly Blue'** bears sky blue flowers with a white center.

Problems & Pests

Morning glories are susceptible to several fungal problems, but they occur only rarely.

I. tricolor cultivar

If 'easy to grow' is your gardening motto, morning glories are for you.

I. batatas 'Margarita'

Musk Mallow

Abelmoschus

Height: 18"– 5' **Spread:** 18–24" **Flower color:** white to yellow with purple centers, red with white centers, pink, orange

THOUGH NOT A STELLAR PERFORMER IN UPPER MIDWEST GARDENS—musk mallows flower most abundantly in regions with long, hot summers—the great novelty of the bloom form and wide range of height options make musk mallow a favorite of northern gardeners in the know. If you're originally from the South, you may know this plant by the common name lady's fingers.

Planting

Seeding: Sow seed indoors in late winter or early spring; direct sow in spring after danger of frost has passed

Planting out: Well after last frost

Spacing: 12–18"

Growing

Musk mallows prefer **full sun**. The soil should be **fertile** and **well drained.** Fertilize monthly for good performance.

Tips

Use musk mallows in an annual or mixed border. The taller types can be used at the back of the border and the lower cultivars in the middle or near the front.

Recommended

A. moschatus (musk mallow) is a bushy perennial that is grown as an annual in cold winter climates. The flowers can be up to 4" across. The seeds have a musky scent. **'Oriental Red'** bears red flowers that fade to white at the centers. **Pacific Series** has compact plants that grow to 18" tall, with flowers in various colors.

Problems & Pests

Musk mallows may have trouble with fungal diseases such as powdery mildew and root rot and with spider mites, slugs and whiteflies.

Abelmoschus *is from the Arabic* abulmosk, *'father of musk,' and like the common name refers to the musk-scented seeds.*

'Oriental Red'

These plants are related to hibiscus, mallow and hollyhock.

A. moschatus

Nasturtium

Tropaeolum

Height: 8–18" for dwarf varieties; up to 10' for trailing varieties **Spread:** equal to or slightly greater than height **Flower color:** red, orange, yellow, pink, cream, gold or bicolored

'EASY TO GROW' IS A PHRASE TOO OFTEN USED BY THE GARDENING industry, but in the case of nasturtiums, it's as accurate as can be. These plants thrive in northern summers; in fact, southern growing conditions featuring intense heat and humidity wipe nasturtium out. Some gardeners object to the way the leaves of some varieties seem to compete for attention with (and sometimes cover) the very attractive flowers, but I've always liked the look. Naturally, plant hybridizers have fixed the problem, if you consider it a problem, by creating hybrids with more extended flowers.

Planting

Seeding: Indoors in late winter; direct sow around last-frost date

Planting out: After last frost

Spacing: 8–12"

Growing

Nasturtiums prefer **full sun** but tolerate some shade. The soil should be of **average to poor fertility, light, moist** and **well drained.** Too rich a soil or too much nitrogen fertilizer will result in lots of leaves and very few flowers. Let the soil drain completely between waterings.

If you start nasturtium seeds indoors, sow them in individual peat pots to avoid disturbing the roots during transplanting.

Tips

Nasturtiums can be used in beds, borders, containers, hanging baskets and on sloped banks. The climbing varieties are grown up trellises or over rock walls or places that need concealing. This plant thrives in poor locations, and it makes an interesting addition to plantings on hard-to-mow slopes.

'Peach Melba'

The painter Claude Monet was a fan of nasturtiums, and he planted the entryway to his home in the south of France with this colorful and edible ornamental.

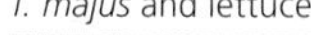

T. majus and lettuce

T. majus (above), Alaska Series (below)

Some gardeners believe that nasturtium attracts and harbors certain pests, such as whiteflies and aphids, so it should not be grown near plants that are susceptible to the same problems. Other gardeners believe that nasturtium is preferred by pest insects and that the pests will flock to it and leave the rest of the garden alone. Still other gardeners claim that the high sulfur levels in the leaves repel many pests that would otherwise infest the garden. Whatever the case, if you do find aphids on your nasturtiums, you will notice that they congregate near the growing tips. Cut the infested parts off and drop them in a bucket of soapy water to rid yourself of this problem.

Recommended

T. majus has a trailing habit. It has been greatly improved by hybridizing. The foliage of the older varieties tended to hide the flowers, but the new varieties hold their flowers—available in a great selection of colors—above the foliage. There are also some new and interesting cultivars with variegated foliage and compact, attractive, mound-forming habits. **Alaska Series** plants have white-marbled foliage and single flowers in shades of yellow, orange, red and cream. **'Empress of India'** grows 8–12" tall and 12–18" wide, with deep crimson flowers and dark purple-blue foliage. **Jewel Series** includes compact plants that grow to 12" tall and wide, with double flowers in a mix of deep orange, red or gold. **'Peach Melba'** forms a 12" mound. The flowers are pale yellow with a bright orange-red splash at the base of each petal. **'Whirlybird'**

is a compact, bushy plant. The single or double flowers in shades of red, pink, yellow or orange do not have spurs.

T. peregrinum (canary bird vine, canary creeper) is a vigorous climber with five-lobed leaves. It grows about 10' tall. The yellow flowers are borne in loose clusters. The two upper petals of each flower are fringed, giving the flowers a bird-like appearance.

Problems & Pests

The few problems that afflict nasturtiums include aphids, slugs, whiteflies and some viruses.

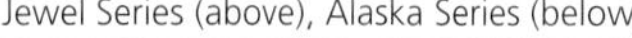

Jewel Series (above), Alaska Series (below)

Nemesia

Nemesia

Height: 6–24" **Spread:** 4–12" **Flower color:** blue, purple, pink, white, red, orange, yellow or bicolored

THOUGH THESE SOUTH AFRICAN NATIVES SOMETIMES FALTER IN excessively hot summers, the relatively cool climate of the upper Midwest is most often beneficial to their growth. This is a superb plant; its bushy form and strong stems pack profuse clusters of flowers, making it perfect for use in containers. It also makes a long-lasting cut flower.

Planting

Seeding: Indoors in early spring

Planting out: After last frost

Spacing: 6"

Growing

Nemesia prefers **full sun.** The soil should be **average to fertile, slightly acidic, moist** and **well drained.** Regular watering will keep this plant blooming through the summer.

Tips

Nemesia makes a bright and colorful addition to the front of a mixed border or mixed container planting.

Recommended

N. caerulea (*N. fruticans*) is a bushy plant that grows up to 24" tall and spreads about 12". It bears blue, pink, purple or white flowers. Several cultivars are available as transplants. **'Blue Bird'** bears lavender blue flowers on plants 8–12" tall. **'Blue Lagoon'** also grows 8–12" tall and produces slate blue flowers. **'Candy Girl'** bears frilled, fragrant, light pink flowers on 10–12" tall plants. **'Compact Innocence'** grows 10–12" tall, and **'Innocence'** grows 12–14" tall; both have fragrant, lilac-scented white flowers. The preceding cultivars can all be planted out in early spring and will tolerate frosts and cool temperatures, but they are also very heat tolerant when fertilized regularly. **Safari Series** includes vigorous plants that grow 8–14" tall, with good heat tolerance and fragrant blooms. In this series, 'Pink' has pink flowers, and 'Plum' features large purple flowers.

N. strumosa forms a bushy mound of bright green foliage. It grows 6–12" tall and spreads 4–8". It bears flowers in shades of blue, purple, white, pink, red or yellow, often in bicolors. **Carnival Series** plants bear many flowers in yellow, white, orange, pink or red on compact plants. **'KLM'** has bicolored blue and white flowers with yellow throats. **'National Ensign'** ('Red and White') bears flowers bicolored red and white.

N. caerulea in a hanging basket

Problems & Pests

Occasional problems with crown or root rot are possible.

'National Ensign'

Ornamental Kale

Brassica

Height: 12–24" **Spread:** 12–24" **Flower color:** grown for foliage

I FIRST SPIED ORNAMENTAL KALE USED IN CONTAINERS A DECADE or so ago, and the novel look of the plant remains as in vogue today as it was then. The plant is grown for its stunning, variegated foliage and is wonderful in containers and flower boxes. If the flower box hangs beneath the kitchen window, you have the added benefit of easily harvesting a few leaves to add color to salads because the entire plant is edible.

Ornamental kale is related to cabbage and broccoli and makes a colorful addition to any salad. The oldest leaves may be somewhat bitter.

Planting

Seeding: Direct sow in spring or indoors in early spring

Planting out: Spring

Spacing: 18–24"

Growing

Ornamental kale prefers to grow in **full sun** but tolerates partial shade. The soil should be **neutral to slightly alkaline, fertile, well drained** and **moist**. For best results, side dress with fertilizer a couple of times through the summer.

Plants can be started in trays and transplanted in spring. Many packages of seeds contain a variety of cultivars.

The plant colors brighten after a light frost or at temperatures below 50° F.

Tips

Ornamental kale is a tough, bold plant at home in both vegetable gardens and flowerbeds.

Wait until some true leaves develop before thinning. Use seedlings you don't transplant in salads.

Recommended

B. oleracea (Acephala Group) forms loose, erect rosettes of large, often fringed leaves in shades of purple, red, pink and white. It grows 12–24" tall and wide. **'Osaka'** grows 12" tall and wide with wavy foliage, red to pink in the center and blue to green to the outside. **'Sunrise'** and **'Sunset'** are new, small-headed, long-stemmed plants used as long-lasting cut flowers. They grow up to 24" tall. The central leaves of 'Sunrise' are creamy white with a pink tinge in the very center. 'Sunset' has red-colored foliage.

Problems & Pests

Ornamental kale is affected by a large range of pests and diseases, including caterpillars, leaf miners, aphids, root maggots, cabbage worm (white butterfly), nematodes, plant bugs, flea beetles, leaf spot, clubroot and damping off. It may also suffer nutrient deficiencies.

Osteospermum

Cape Daisy, African Daisy

Osteospermum

Height: 10–20" **Spread:** 10–20" **Flower color:** white, peach, orange, yellow, pink, purple, red; often with dark centers of blue-purple or other colors

OF THE MANY ANNUALS FEATURING DAISY-LIKE FLOWERS, osteospermum is my favorite. Most cultivars feature muted shades of color that give the plant a subtle elegance. Osteospermum is outstanding when massed in the garden bed but possesses an assured and stately nature that allows plants placed singly to hold their own. I use it as the centerpiece in mixed containers as well and cannot imagine a summer without growing it.

Planting

Seeding: Indoors in early spring

Planting out: Late April or May; plants can withstand light frosts if hardened off

Spacing: 10–18"

Growing

Plant in **full sun** in **light, evenly moist, moderately fertile, well-drained** soil. Do not overwater or let the plants wilt. Feed weekly with a well-balanced, water-soluble fertilizer that is high in nitrogen to keep them flowering all summer long. Use an organic mulch to cut down on the plants' water needs. Deadhead to encourage new growth and more flowers. Pinch young plants to encourage bushiness.

Tips

The genus *Osteospermum* includes tender perennials and subshrubs from South Africa that we use as annuals. Recent breeding efforts have made these plants much more likely to thrive in our northern gardens. Use them in containers or

O. ecklonis 'Passion Mix'

Many Osteospermum *will tolerate winter temperatures as low as 14°F in open areas.*

O. 'Cream Symphony' and O. 'Orange Symphony'

O. 'Lemon Symphony'

The genus name Osteospermum *arises from the Greek words* osteon, *'bone,' and* sperma, *'seed,' because its seeds are hard and bone-like in texture and color.*

beds, and their daisy flowers look great mixed with plants such as petunia or verbena.

Recommended

O. ecklonis is a variable subshrub that can grow upright to almost prostrate. The species is almost never grown in favor of its wonderful cultivars. **Passion Mix** includes free-flowering, heat-tolerant plants growing 12" tall and 10" wide. The flowers come in pink, rose, purple and pure white, and have deep blue centers. This series was an All-America Selections winner in 1999. **Springstar Series** is a group of compact, early-flowering plants that include the following five cultivars: 'Arctur' grows 14–16" tall and wide and produces white flowers; 'Aurora' grows 10–13" tall and wide and bears magenta to lavender flowers; 'Capella' is heat tolerant and grows 14–16" tall and wide with large white flowers; 'Mira' grows 14–16" tall and wide and produces purple to deep magenta flowers with good heat tolerance; 'Sirius' bears magenta

O. ecklonis Starwhirls Series

to deep red flowers with elongated petals and grows 18–20" in height and spread. **Starwhirls Series** plants grow 12–18" tall and wide. They have unique spoon-shaped petals. Included in this series are 'Antaris,' which bears deep pink flowers, and 'Vega,' whose petals are white on the upper surface and dusky pink beneath.

***O.* Symphony Series** from Proven Winners are mounding plants growing 10–15" tall and wide. They are very heat tolerant and flower well through the summer. **'Cream'** has cream flowers. **'Lemon'** has lemon yellow flowers. **'Orange'** grows slightly smaller and has wonderful tangerine orange flowers. **'Peach'** bears lightly flushed peachy pink flowers. **'Vanilla'** bears white flowers.

Problems & Pests

Osteospermum may experience problems with downy mildew, *Verticillium* wilt and aphids. Fungal diseases may occur in hot, rainy summers or if plants are overwatered.

O. ecklonis

You may find these plants listed as either Osteospermum *or* Dimorphotheca. *The latter is a closely related genus that formerly included all the plants now listed as* Osteospermum.

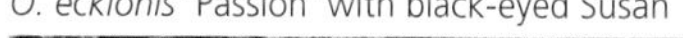

O. ecklonis 'Passion' with black-eyed Susan

Painted-Tongue

Velvet Flower

Salpiglossis

Height: up to 24" **Spread:** 12" **Flower color:** red, blue, yellow, orange, purple, brown; often patterned bicolors

PAINTED-TONGUE IS AN UP-AND-COMING FIRECRACKER OF A flower being found at more and more nurseries across our two states. The tongue-shaped flower petals curl backward and are borne in great profusion from early summer into fall. Most blooms feature wildly veined, bicolor combinations that are sure to attract attention. Its only shortfall is a tendency to fail in mid-summer heat, so grow it where it receives a break from intense, midday sun. A single plant grown in a mid-sized container adds riotous focal point to the deck or patio.

Planting

Seeding: Indoors in late winter; direct sow in spring

Planting out: After last frost

Spacing: 8–12"

Growing

Painted-tongue prefers **full sun.** The soil should be **fertile,** rich in **organic matter** and **well drained.** A location sheltered from heavy rain and wind will keep these plants looking their best.

As with many members of the potato family, the seeds of painted-tongue are very tiny and shouldn't be covered with soil. They will germinate more evenly if kept in darkness until they sprout. Once they start to sprout, move the plants to a well-lit location.

The iridescent quality of these flowers causes their color to change as they turn in a breeze.

Tips

Painted-tongue is useful in the middle or back of beds and borders. It can also be added to large mixed containers. Most types of painted-tongue can become battered in rain and wind, so plant in a warm, sheltered area of the garden.

Recommended

S. sinuata is an upright plant in the same family as petunias. **'Blue Peacock'** has blue flowers with yellow throats and dark veins. Plants of the **Casino Series,** with flowers in a wide range of colors, bloom early and tolerate rain and wind. The **Royale Series** has flowers with more pronounced veining in the throat. 'Royale Chocolate' ('Chocolate Pot') has chocolate brown flowers. 'Royale Mixed' bears solid and bicolor flowers in blue, chocolate, deep red, orange, pale blue, purple, red and yellow.

Problems & Pests

Occasional problems with aphids or root rot are possible.

Pentas

Star Clusters, Egyptian Star

Pentas

Height: 12–24" **Spread:** 12–24" **Flower color:** pink, red, purple, white

THIS FLORIFEROUS ANNUAL IS BECOMING INCREASINGLY POPULAR at nurseries across both states, and it is a noteworthy addition to the northern garden. Large clusters of star-shaped flowers are borne in mounds that often cover the entire plant. The dense, shiny, somewhat coarse foliage provides a nice foil to the overall daintiness of the flower. Use pentas to provide season-long color in the mixed annual/perennial garden.

Planting

Seeding: Indoors in late winter or direct sow in spring

Planting out: Around last frost date

Spacing: 10–20"

Growing

Pentas grows best in **full sun** and **well-drained, moist, fertile** soil. Ensure you provide adequate water. Propagate plants from seed or softwood cuttings in summer. Regular deadheading will encourage more blooms.

Tips

Use pentas in a bed or border where the coarse foliage provides a backdrop for smaller plants at the front of the border. Pentas also does very well as an outdoor container plant and is often sold during winter as a houseplant. Cuttings can be taken from houseplants and grown outside the following summer.

Recommended

P. lanceolata is a subshrub grown as an annual. It has an erect, sometimes prostrate, growth habit and produces flat-topped clusters of star-shaped pink, red, purple or white flowers in summer. **'Avalanche'** bears white flowers and has variegated foliage. **'Kermesiana'** bears red-throated fuchsia pink flowers. **'New Look White'** is a vigorous, compact plant growing 12–15" tall and bearing clusters of white flowers.

Problems & Pests

Aphids and spider mites may cause problems. Check the plants carefully when purchasing.

P. lanceolata (photos this page)

Pinch back the tips for a more compact, bushier plant.

Petunia

Petunia

Height: 6–18" **Spread:** 12–24" or more **Flower color:** pink, purple, red, white, coral, blue or bicolored

LONG AN OLD-FASHIONED MAINSTAY OF THE AMERICAN FLOWER garden, grandma's dear petunias have received a real shot of adrenaline with the recent introduction of the trailing 'Wave' and 'Surfinia' Series, to the point where the plant is selling like never before. Wave Series petunias are the ones you see in breathtaking hanging baskets at the nursery, and Surfinia Series plants are superb in flower boxes and pots. Most newer varieties do not require the excessive deadheading that made the maintenance of petunias a chore, though thorough deadheading at least once a week remains a good idea.

With the introduction of many wonderful new varieties, petunias may again outrank impatiens as America's most popular bedding plants.

Planting

Seeding: Indoors in mid-winter

Planting out: After last frost

Spacing: 8–18"

Growing

Petunias prefer **full sun.** The soil should be of **average to rich fertility, light, sandy** and **well drained.** When sowing, press seeds into the soil surface but don't cover them with soil. Pinch halfway back in mid-summer to keep plants bushy and to encourage new growth and flowers.

Tips

Use petunias in beds, borders, containers and hanging baskets.

Recommended

P.* x *hybrida is a large group of popular, sun-loving annuals that fall into three categories: grandifloras, multifloras and millifloras.

The **grandiflora** petunias have the largest flowers—up to 4" across. They have the widest variety of colors and forms, but they are the most likely to be damaged by heavy rain.

'Merlin Blue Morn'

The name Petunia *is derived from 'petun,' the Brazilian word for tobacco, which comes from the species of the related genus* Nicotiana.

Fantasy Series

'Tidal Wave Silver' (above), milliflora type (below)

Daddy Series plants are available in darkly veined shades of pink and purple. **'Merlin Blue Morn,'** an All-America Selections winner, bears blue and white bicolored flowers that are white in the center and fade to velvety blue at the petal edges. **Supercascade Series** plants come in a wide variety of colors. Cultivars in the **Ultra Series** are available in many colors, including bicolors, and recover quite quickly from weather damage.

Compared to the grandifloras, the **multiflora** petunias have smaller blooms (about half the size), bear many more flowers and tolerate adverse weather conditions better. **Carpet Series** has plants in a wide variety of colors. Petunias in the **Surfinia Series** branch freely, are self-cleaning and form a neat mound covered by a mass of flowers in shades of pink, blue, purple and white. Look for new additions to the series, which feature double flowers, minis, pastel colors and decorative veining. **Wave Series** plants have flowers in pink, purple or coral. The low, spreading habit makes this series popular as a groundcover and for hanging baskets and containers. The plants recover well from rain damage, bloom nonstop, tolerate cold and spread quickly.

The **milliflora** petunias are the newest group. The flowers are about 1" across and are borne profusely over the whole plant. These plants tolerate wet weather very well and sometimes self-seed. They are popular in mixed containers and hanging baskets and are also very nice in garden beds, forming neat mounds of foliage and flowers. **Fantasy Series** is available in shades of red, purple, pink and white although the pinks tend to be easiest to find. **Supertunia Mini Series** varieties bear small, weather-resistant blue, pink, lilac, purple or white flowers on well-branched plants. Some of the flowers in this series have darkened veins on the petals. With the growing popularity of the millifloras, more colors will very likely become available.

Problems & Pests

Aphids and fungi may present problems. Fungal problems can be avoided by wetting the foliage as little as possible and by providing a location with good drainage.

'Blue Wave' (above), 'Lavender Wave' (center)

Ultra Series (below)

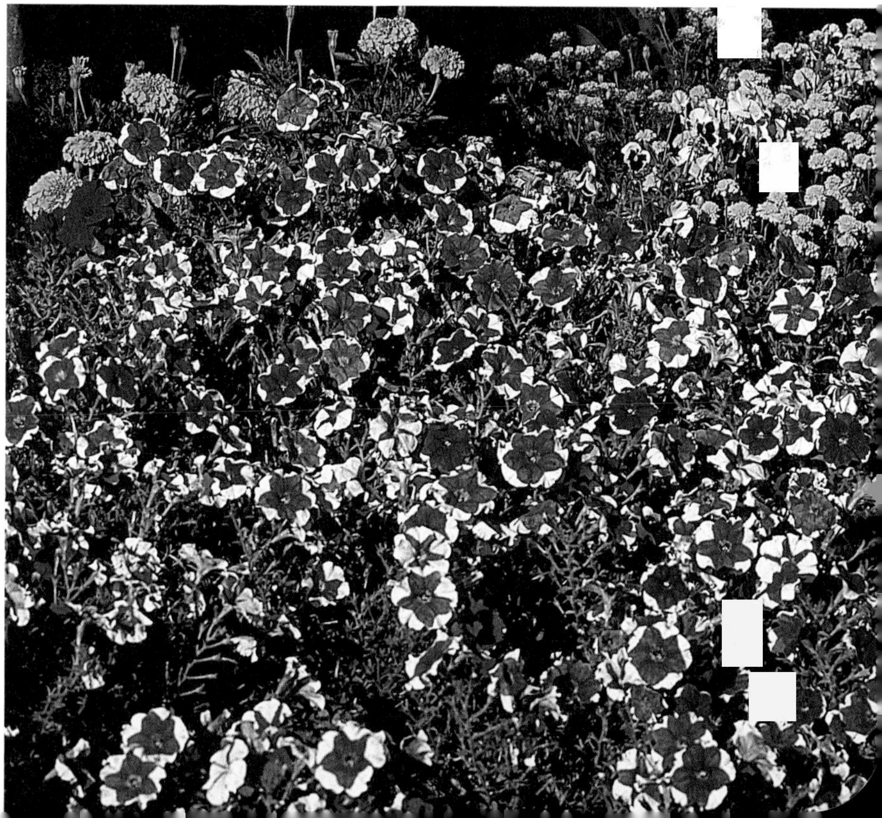

Pimpernel

Anagallis

Height: 6–18" **Spread:** 8–18" **Flower color:** red, white, blue, pink

FEW GROUND-HUGGING ANNUALS PACK AS POWERFUL A PUNCH as pimpernel. This diminutive annual produces masses of flowers throughout summer, making it useful as an edging plant as well as in large, informal areas. Newer hybrids have expanded the palette to include orange, white and pink flowers. In parts of Europe, blue pimpernel is called poor-man's weatherglass, a reference to the tendency of its flowers to close on cloudy days.

Planting

Seeding: Start indoors in late winter

Planting out: Around the last frost date

Spacing: 6–16"

Growing

Pimpernel prefers **full sun.** The soil should be **fertile, moist** and **well drained.** This plant does not tolerate compacted or clay soils.

Tips

These low-growing plants make a colorful addition to the front of a border. They are useful in a new rock garden where slower-growing alpine plants have not yet filled in.

Be careful when handling these plants; touching the leaves may cause a skin rash.

Recommended

A. ***arvensis*** (scarlet pimpernel) is a low, trailing plant that grows up to 6" tall and spreads up to 18". It bears red or white flowers that close on cloudy days and at night. This species prefers cool weather and may stop flowering in summer.

A. ***monellii*** (blue pimpernel) is a low-growing, somewhat upright plant. It grows 8–18" tall, with an equal spread, and bears blue, white, pink or red flowers. This species prefers warm weather. **'Skylover'** is an upright plant from Proven Winners. It bears deep blue flowers, which are larger that those of the species.

Problems & Pests

Aphids can be a problem.

A. monellii 'Skylover'

Pimpernels are in the same family as primroses.

A. monellii 'Skylover' with sweet alyssum

Pincushion Flower

Scabiosa

Scabiosa

Height: 18–36" **Spread:** up to 12" **Flower color:** purple, blue, maroon, pink, white, red, bronze

SEVERAL SPECIES OF ANNUAL PINCUSHION FLOWER PERFORM extremely well in northern gardens and include some that are wonderfully scented. The rather rag-tag appearance of the bloom form brings comfortable charm to the cottage garden and other loose, informal environments. This plant does not put on airs. In the garden, plant it next to annuals and perennials featuring prominent foliage, since the plant's own foliage is nondescript at best. This is an excellent flower for cutting.

Planting

Seeding: Indoors in late winter; direct sow in mid-spring

Planting out: After last frost

Spacing: 8–12"

Growing

Pincushion flowers grow best in **full sun**. The soil should be of **average to rich fertility, alkaline, well drained** and rich in **organic matter**. Keep the soil moderately moist, but do not overwater.

Tips

Pincushion flowers are useful in beds, borders and mixed containers. The flowers are also popular in fresh arrangements.

The tall stems of *S. atropurpurea* may fall over as the plants mature. Insert twiggy branches, often called pea sticks, into the ground around the plants when they are small to give them support as they grow.

Recommended

S. atropurpurea is an upright, branching plant growing up to 36" tall and spreading about 12". The species has purple or crimson flowers; cultivars can come in white or blue as well. **'Ace of Spades'** has deep maroon flowers with a honey scent; it grows to 24" tall. **'Imperial Giants'** bears blooms in a deep maroon as well as shades of pink.

S. stellata grows 18" tall and spreads half as much. This plant bears small white flowers but is grown for its papery, orb-like seedpods, which dry in unusual globe shapes and are useful accents in dried arrangements. Pick *S. stellata* while still slightly green to keep the dried seedpods from shattering. **'Drumstick'** bears blue flowers. The seedpods dry to a warm bronze color. **'Paper Moon'** seedpods dry to a light sky blue.

S. a. 'Imperial Giants'

The name Scabiosa *is related to 'scabies,' which the plant was once thought to cure.*

S. atropurpurea

Polka Dot Plant

Hypoestes

Height: 12–24" **Spread:** 8–12" **Flower color:** purple, inconspicuous; plant grown for pink-, red- or white-spotted leaves

POLKA DOT PLANT IS ENJOYING CURRENT POPULARITY AS A foliage plant as gardeners become increasingly aware that varied, attractive foliage is a key component of good garden design. No need to grow it from seed; it will be available at nurseries near you. I grow tons in mixed containers, and while a sucker for the pink- and red-leaved varieties, I find the primarily white-leafed hybrids useful in combination with any mid-sized annuals sporting yellow or blue blooms.

Planting

Seeding: Indoors in early spring

Planting out: After last-frost date

Spacing: 8–10"

Growing

Polka dot plant prefers **full sun** but tolerates light shade. Too much shade will reduce leaf coloration and can encourage floppy growth. The soil should be of **average fertility, humus rich, moist** and **well drained**.

Pinch growing tips frequently to encourage bushy growth. Pinch off the inconspicuous flowers or the plants may decline.

Tips

Polka dot plants can be used in small groups as accent plants, in mass plantings and in mixed containers. In general, because this plant is small, it looks best planted in clusters rather than singly.

Recommended

H. phyllostachya (*H. sanguinolenta*) is a bushy plant grown for its attractive foliage. This species has mostly green leaves that are lightly dusted with pink spots. Several cultivars have been developed with more dramatic foliage. Plants in the **Confetti Series** have foliage that is heavily spotted with light or dark pink or white. **Splash Series** plants have foliage that is brightly streaked and spotted with pink, white or red.

Problems & Pests

This plant is usually problem free, but rare instances of powdery mildew can occur.

Splash Series

Polka dot plant is often grown as a houseplant and does best in a sunny window.

Confetti Series

Poor Man's Orchid

Butterfly Flower

Schizanthus

Height: 6–18" **Spread:** 8–12" **Flower color:** pink, red, orange, yellow, white, purple; yellow throats are marked with contrasting streaks and blotches

THIS NATIVE OF CHILE IS AN EXCELLENT ADDITION TO NORTHERN gardens, where it flourishes in our relatively cool summers. Upright stems bearing profuse, veined and blotched blooms in a wide range of colors are nicely offset by pale green, fern-like foliage. Poor man's orchid is a great plant for the front of the bed, but you will need to replace it with something else in August, after it completes its colorful show.

Planting

Seeding: Indoors 4–8 weeks before last frost; direct sow around last frost date

Planting out: After last frost

Spacing: 8–12"

Growing

Poor man's orchid grows best in **full sun** to **partial shade** and appreciates some relief from the hot afternoon sun. The soil should be **fertile, moist** and **well drained.** This plant does not tolerate frost or excess heat and also does quite well planted in light shade.

The seeds should be planted on the soil surface. Keep the entire container in darkness or cover it with dark plastic or newspaper to promote even germination. When sowing directly, use a row cover to give the plants a head start. Remove the cover once the seeds have sprouted.

These plants have a short flowering season, but you can extend the bloom time with successive sowings. Alternatively, you can replace them halfway through summer with chrysanthemums that bloom in late summer and fall.

The flowers of poor man's orchid are colorful and long lasting after they are cut, making them a good choice for fresh arrangements.

Tips

Poor man's orchid can be used in beds, borders, rock gardens, hanging baskets and mixed containers. It does best in cool summer climates. This plant combines well with creeping zinnia (*Sanvitalia*) and most other annuals.

Poor man's orchid can be grown as a temporary indoor potted plant in a bright, sunny window. Don't over-water plants indoors, and never put a tray containing water underneath the plant.

Recommended

S. **'Angel Wings'** is a trailing hybrid 12–18" tall and 8–12" wide. Flower colors range from pale pink to lavender to deep violet, all with darker veining and golden yellow throats. These are excellent plants for hanging baskets and containers.

S. pinnatus is an erect plant with light green, fern-like leaves. The brightly colored flowers bloom for an extended period from spring to fall. **'Disco'** is a hybrid with *S. pinnatus* as one of the parents. These compact plants grow 6–9" tall and bear a profusion of flowers in mixed colors. **Dwarf Bouquet Mixed** plants are shorter and more compact, growing to 16" tall. They make good container plants and have flowers in shades of red, orange, pink and orange-yellow. **Royal Pierrot Mixed** plants have rich colors in pink, purple, purple-blue and white and are good in hanging baskets. **'Star Parade'** is a compact variety available in several colors. It grows up to 10" tall.

The genus name Schizanthus *arises from the Greek words* schizo, *meaning 'to cut,' and* anthos, *meaning 'flower,' referring to the deeply cut flower petals.*

Poppy

Papaver

Height: 12"–4' **Spread:** 8–12" **Flower color:** red, pink, white, purple, yellow, orange

ANNUAL POPPIES RESEMBLE THEIR PERENNIAL BRETHREN TO such an extent that some gardeners grow the annual instead of fussing with the perennial. Given a sunny site and well-drained soil, your garden will be inundated with festive, brightly colored blooms. Because of their relatively short, early summer bloom period, it's best to grow poppies as filler for large areas such as meadows, informal borders and cottage gardens.

Planting

Seeding: Direct sow every two weeks in spring

Spacing: 10–12"

Growing

Poppies grow best in **full sun**. The soil should be **fertile** and **sandy** and have lots of **organic matter** mixed in. Good drainage is essential. If you choose to start your seeds indoors, they must be in peat pots or peat pellets. However, seedlings really do not like having their roots disturbed, so transplanting is often unsuccessful. Mix the tiny seeds with fine sand for even sowing. Do not cover, because the seeds need light to germinate. Deadhead to prolong blooming.

Tips

Poppies work well in mixed borders where other plants are slow to fill in. The poppies will fill in empty spaces early in the season then die back over the summer, leaving room for other plants. They can also be used in rock gardens, and the cut flowers are popular for fresh arrangements.

Be careful when weeding around faded summer plants; you may accidentally pull up germinating poppy seedlings.

The large seed capsules of opium poppy can be dried and used in floral arrangements.

Recommended

P. nudicaule (Iceland poppy) is a short-lived perennial that is grown as an annual. It grows 12–18" tall

The use of poppy seeds in cooking and baking can be traced as far back as the ancient Egyptians.

P. nudicaule

P. rupifragum

and spreads about 12". Red, orange, yellow, pink or white flowers appear in spring and early summer. This plant tends to self-seed, but it will gradually disappear from the garden if it is left to its own devices. **'Champagne Bubbles'** bears 3" wide flowers in solid and bicolored shades of red, orange and yellow.

P. rhoeas (Flanders poppy, field poppy, corn poppy) forms a basal rosette of foliage above which the flowers are borne on long stems. **'Mother of Pearl'** bears flowers in pastel pinks and purples. **Shirley Series** (Shirley poppy) flowers have silky, cup-shaped petals. The flowers come in many colors and may be single, semi-double or double.

P. rupifragum (Spanish poppy) is a perennial from Spain that can be grown as an annual. It grows 18" tall and 8–10" wide and produces pale brick red to orange flowers over a long period in summer.

These fleeting beauties will not interfere with later-blooming perennials. Simply remove the spent poppies as they decline.

P. rhoeas Shirley Series

P. somniferum (opium poppy) grows up to 4' tall. The flowers are red, pink, white or purple. This plant has a mixed reputation. Its milky sap is the source of several drugs, including codeine, morphine and opium. All parts of the plant can cause stomach upset and even coma except for the seeds, which are a popular culinary additive (poppy seeds). The seeds contain only minute amounts of the chemicals that make this plant pharmaceutically valuable. Though propagation of the species is restricted in many countries, several attractive cultivars have been developed for ornamental use. **'Danebrog Lace'** originated in the 19th century. The single flowers have frilly, red petals with a large, white patch at the base of each petal. **'Hens and Chickens'** bears large flowers and large, decorative seedheads. Each large seedhead is surrounded by numerous smaller

P. s. 'Hens and Chickens'

seedheads, like a mother hen surrounded by her chicks. **'Peony Flowered'** has large, frilly, double flowers in a variety of colors on plants that grow up to 36" in height.

Problems & Pests

Poppies rarely have problems although fungi may be troublesome if the soil is wet and poorly drained.

For cut flowers, seal the cut end of each stem with a flame or boiling water.

P. somniferum 'Peony Flowered'

Portulaca

Moss Rose

Portulaca

Height: 4–8" **Spread:** 6–12" or more **Flower color:** red, pink, yellow, white, cream, purple, orange, peach

PORTULACA IS A LONGTIME FAVORITE OF GARDENERS LOOKING TO add intense color to dry areas along sidewalks and driveways. It's best grown in clumps or waves of five or more plants. The plant's small stature, need for intense sun and preference for sandy soils make it a natural in rock gardens. While it does not tolerate foot traffic, I've seen it planted between the cracks of patio stone to dramatic effect. Its blooms are so colorful that when people see it, they walk around it.

Planting

Seeding: Indoors in late winter

Planting out: Once soil has warmed

Spacing: 12"

Growing

Portulacas require **full sun**. The soil should be of **poor fertility, sandy** and **well drained**. To ensure that you will have plants where you want them, start seed indoors. If you sow directly outdoors, the tiny seeds may get washed away by rain and the plants will pop up in unexpected places. Spacing the plants close together is not a problem; in fact, it results in well-mixed flower colors.

Tips

Portulacas are the ideal plants for spots that just don't get enough water—under the eaves of the house or in dry, rocky, exposed areas. They are also ideal for people who like baskets hanging from the front porch but who always forget to water them. As long as the location is sunny, these plants will do well with minimal care.

Recommended

P. grandiflora forms a bushy mound of succulent foliage. It bears delicate, papery, rose-like flowers profusely all summer. **'Cloudbeater'** bears large, double flowers in many colors. The flowers stay open all day, even in cloudy weather. **Margarita Series** plants have semi-double flowers in white, cream, yellow, orange, pink and red. All-America Selections winner 'Margarita Rosita' has deep pink flowers. **Sundial Series** plants have long-lasting, double flowers. AAS winner 'Sundial Peach' has double flowers in shades of peach.

Problems & Pests

If portulacas have excellent drainage and as much light as possible, they shouldn't have problems.

With only minimal attention, portulacas will fill a sunny, exposed strip of soil next to pavement with bright colors all summer.

Salvia

Sage

Salvia

Height: 12"–4' **Spread:** 8"–4' **Flower color:** red, blue, purple, burgundy, pink, orange, salmon, yellow, cream, white, bicolored

WISCONSIN AND MINNESOTA GARDENERS KNOW A GOOD ANNUAL when they see it, and that's why salvia has become such a popular mainstay of beds, borders and containers across the two great states. Salvia comprises a large group of plants, many with exciting new cultivars to choose from. Regardless of height or bloom color, what most salvias bring to the garden is season-long bloom via strong, vertical stature.

Planting

Seeding: Indoors in mid-winter; direct sow in spring

Planting out: After last frost

Spacing: 8–10"

Growing

All salvias prefer **full sun** but tolerate light shade. The soil should be **moist, well drained** and of **average to rich fertility**, with lots of **organic matter**.

To keep plants producing flowers, water often and fertilize monthly. Remove spent flowers before they begin to turn brown.

Tips

Salvias look good grouped in beds, borders and containers. The blooms are long lasting and make lovely cut flowers for arrangements.

Recommended

S. argentea (silver sage) is grown for its large, fuzzy, silvery leaves. It grows up to 36" tall, spreads about

S. coccinea 'Coral Nymph'

The long-lasting flowers of salvias hold up well in adverse weather.

S. splendens and *S. farinacea* with lobelia

S. viridis

The genus name Salvia *comes from the Latin* salvus, *'save,' referring to the medicinal properties of several species.*

S. farinacea 'Victoria'

24" and bears small, white or pink-tinged flowers. This plant is a biennial or short-lived perennial grown as an annual.

S. coccinea (bloody sage, Texas sage) grows 24–30" tall and 12" wide and bears dark pink flowers. **'Coral Nymph'** grows 12–20" tall and has bicolored salmon and white flowers. **'Forest Fire'** has red flowers tinged with black on well-branched plants 12–24" tall. **'Lady in Red,'** an All-America Selections winner, grows 12–18" tall and bears red, trumpet-shaped blooms in rings around the flower spike.

S. elegans (*S. rutilans*; pineapple sage) is a large, bushy plant with soft leaves and bright red flowers. It grows 3–4' tall, with an equal spread. The foliage smells of pineapple when crushed and is used as a culinary flavoring.

S. farinacea (mealy cup sage, blue sage) has bright blue flowers clustered along stems powdered with silver. The plant grows up to 24" tall, with a spread of 12". The flowers are also available in white. **'Strata,'** an All-America Selections winner, has bicolored blue and white flowers. **'Victoria'** is a popular cultivar with silvery foliage and deep blue flowers that make a beautiful addition to cut-flower arrangements.

S. patens (gentian sage) bears vivid blue flowers on plants 18–24" tall. This plant is a tender perennial grown as an annual. Being tuberous-rooted, it can be lifted and brought inside for winter in the same way as dahlias. **'Cambridge Blue'** bears pale blue flowers.

S. splendens (salvia, scarlet sage) grows 12–18" tall and spreads up to 12". It is known for its spikes of bright red, tubular flowers. Recently, cultivars have become available in white, pink, purple and orange. **'Phoenix'** forms a neat, compact plant with flowers in many bright and pastel shades. **'Salsa'** bears solid or bicolored flowers in shades of red, orange, purple, burgundy, cream or pink. **Sizzler Series** includes plants with flowers in burgundy, lavender, pink, plum, red, salmon or white and salmon bicolor. **'Vista'** is an early-flowering, compact plant with dark blue-green foliage and bright red flowers.

S. viridis (*S. horminum;* annual clary sage) is grown for its colorful bracts (modified leaves). It grows 18–24" tall, with a spread of 8–12". **'Claryssa'** grows 18" tall and has bracts in pink, purple, blue or white. **'Oxford Blue'** bears purple-blue bracts.

S. elegans

Problems & Pests

Seedlings are prone to damping-off. Aphids and a few fungal problems may trouble adult plants.

S. farinacea 'Victoria' with phlox

Snapdragon

Antirrhinum

Height: 6"–4' **Spread:** 6–20" **Flower color:** white, cream, yellow, orange, red, pink, purple, bronze, bicolored

THE ROUNDED, PLAYFUL SPIRES OF PASTEL flowers that define the snapdragon have been popular in the northern U.S. almost since the land was settled. Snapdragons are ancient and have been cultivated in their native Mediterranean region for centuries. You'll find dozens of ready-to-plant varieties at nurseries, including new, taller varieties (Rocket Series) that allow placement at the back of the border. They are also among the best plants around for containers.

Snapdragons are extremely sensitive to gravity, a phenomenon known as geotropism. When they are held in a horizontal position, they quickly turn upward.

Planting

Seeding: Indoors in late winter; direct sow in spring

Planting out: After last frost

Spacing: 6–18"

Growing

Snapdragons prefer **full sun** but tolerate light or partial shade. The soil should be **fertile,** rich in **organic matter** and **well drained.** Snapdragons prefer a **neutral** or **alkaline** soil and will not perform as well in acidic soil. Do not cover seeds when sowing, because they require light for germination.

To encourage bushier growth, pinch the tips of the plants while they are young. Cut off the flower spikes as they fade to promote further blooming and to prevent the plant from dying back before the end of the season.

Tips

The height of the variety dictates the best place for it in a border—the shortest varieties work well near the front, and the tallest look good in the center or back. The dwarf and medium-height varieties can also be used in planters, and the trailing varieties do well in hanging baskets.

Snapdragons are perennials grown as annuals. They can tolerate cold nights well into fall and may survive a mild winter. Self-sowed seedlings may sprout the following spring if plants are left in place over winter, but because most snapdragons are hybrids they will not come true to type.

Recommended

Many cultivars of *A. majus* are available. Snapdragons are grouped into four classes: dwarf, medium, giant and trailing.

Dwarf varieties grow up to 12" tall. **'Floral Showers'** is a true dwarf, growing 6–8" tall. This plant bears flowers in a wide range of solid colors and bicolors. **'Lampion'** is a new and interesting cultivar, usually grouped with the semi-dwarfs. It has a trailing habit and cascades up to 36", making it a great plant for hanging baskets. **'Princess'** bears white and purple bicolored flowers. This plant produces many shoots from the base and therefore many flower spikes. **Tahiti Series** plants are compact, resist rust and bloom in red, orange, rose pink, bronze or pink and white bicolor.

Snapdragons are interesting and long lasting in fresh flower arrangements. The buds will continue to mature and open even after the spike is cut from the plant.

Medium snapdragons grow 12–24" tall. **'Black Prince'** bears striking, dark purple-red flowers set against bronze-green foliage. **'Crown Candycorn'** grows to 14" tall and bears red and yellow bicolored flowers. **'Jamaican Mist'** plants bear open, trumpet-shaped flowers in cinnamon, shell pink, yellow, apricot, rose or peach on plants up to 15" tall. Plants in the **Ribbon Series** reach 18–24" in height. These early-blooming cultivars include 'Crimson,' 'Lavender,' 'Light Pink,' 'Purple,' 'Rose,' 'White,' 'Yellow' and a mix of the seven different colors. **Sonnet Series** plants grow to 36" tall and are attractive as cut flowers and in the garden.

Giant or tall cultivars can grow 3–4' tall. **'Madame Butterfly'** bears double flowers in a wide range of colors. The flowers of this cultivar are open-faced with a ruffled edge, and they don't 'snap' because the hinged, mouth-like structure has been lost with the addition of the extra petals. Plants in the **Rocket Series** produce long spikes of brightly colored flowers in many shades. They have good heat tolerance.

Trailing snapdragons are excellent for containers and hanging baskets. Plants in the **Luminaire Series** from Ball Seed Co. are vigorous and well branched, reaching 12" in height and 16–20" in spread when grown in a 10" diameter container. The series includes 'Bronze and Yellow,' 'Deep Purple,' 'Deep Yellow,' 'Hot Pink,' 'Orange and Yellow,' 'Pink and White' and 'Yellow.'

Problems & Pests

Snapdragons can suffer from several fungal problems, including powdery and downy mildew, fungal leaf spot, root rot and wilt. Snapdragon rust is the worst. To prevent rust, avoid wetting the foliage, choose varieties that are rust resistant and plant snapdragons in different parts of the garden each year. Aphids may also be troublesome.

Snapdragons can handle cold weather, so they are a good choice for gardeners who can't wait until the last-frost date to plant their annuals.

Statice

Limonium

Height: 12–24" **Spread:** 6–12" **Flower color:** blue, purple, pink, white, yellow, red, orange

PRIZED FOR ITS USE IN DRIED FLOWER ARRANGEMENTS, STATICE is a fine plant for the garden. Plant it in large clumps or waves across informal beds and cottage gardens. No one will know what it is and all will ask. Statice combines beautifully with ageratum, verbena, baby's breath, celosia and nicotiana.

Also known as sea lavender, statice is native to the Mediterranean and grows well in dry, saline habitats.

Planting

Seeding: Indoors in mid-winter; direct sow in spring

Planting out: After last frost

Spacing: 6–12"

Growing

Statice prefers **full sun**. The soil should be of **poor** or **average fertility, light, sandy** and **well drained**. This plant doesn't like having its roots disturbed, so if starting it indoors, use peat pots.

Tips

Statice makes an interesting addition to any sunny border, particularly in informal gardens. It is a perennial grown as an annual.

The basal leaves of statice form a rosette, and the flower stalks are sent up from the middle of the plant. Space the plants quite close together to make up for this lack of width.

Cut statice for drying late in summer, before the white center has come out on the bloom. Stand the stalks in a vase with about 1" of water, and they will dry quite nicely on their own as the water is used up. If it's more convenient to keep them out of the way, you can hang them upside down in a cool, dry place.

Recommended

L. sinuatum forms a basal rosette of hairy leaves. Ridged stems bear clusters of small, papery flowers in blue, purple, pink or white. **'Fortress'** has strongly branching plants and flowers in several bright and pastel shades. The plants grow up to 24" tall. **Petite Bouquet Series** includes compact 12" tall plants with flowers in blue, purple, pink, white and yellow. **'Sunset'** grows 24" tall and bears flowers in warm red, orange, peach, yellow, apricot and salmon shades.

Problems & Pests

Most problems can be avoided by providing a well-drained site and ensuring that there is good air circulation around the plants.

Statice can make an appealing temporary hedge in dry areas of the garden where color is often lacking.

Stock

Matthiola

Height: 8–36" **Spread:** 12" **Flower color:** pink, purple, red, rose, yellow, white

THOUGH STOCK DOES NOT BLOOM FOR LONG, IT PUTS ON SUCH a wonderful, profuse display of flowers beginning in mid-summer that it is well worth your consideration. This plant is not often found as a transplant at northern nurseries, but it is easily grown from seed. Flowers are heavily scented and perfectly presented from attractive, gray-green foliage that may appear silvery in some gardens. Stock combines well with zinnia, larkspur, mallow and cosmos.

When cutting stock flowers for arrangements, cut and then crush the ends of the woody stems so they will draw water more easily.

Planting

Seeding: Indoors in mid-winter or direct sow around last-frost date. Do not cover seeds because they require light to germinate.

Planting out: After last frost

Spacing: 8–12"

Growing

Stock plants prefer **full sun** but tolerate partial shade. The soil should be of **average fertility**, have lots of **organic matter** worked in and be **moist** but **well drained.**

Tips

Stocks can be used in mixed beds or in mass plantings.

Night-scented stock should be planted where its wonderful scent can be enjoyed in the evening—near windows that are left open, beside patios or along pathways. It is best to group night-scented stock with other plants because it tends to look wilted and bedraggled during the day but revives impressively at night.

Recommended

M. incana (stock) is the parent of many cultivar groups. Flower colors range from pink and purple to red, rose or white. The height can be 8–36", depending on the cultivar. **Cinderella Series** is popular. The compact plants in this series grow about 10" tall and have fragrant flowers in a variety of colors. Plants in the **Excelsior Mammoth Column Series** are large, growing about 36" tall and spreading about 12". The flower spikes are up to 12" long, bearing double flowers of red, pink, light purple, pale yellow or white.

M. i. Cinderella Series (photos this page)

M. longipetala **subsp.** ***bicornis*** (night-scented stock, evening-scented stock) has pink or purple flowers and grows 12–18" tall. **'Starlight Scentsation'** bears very fragrant flowers in a wide range of colors.

Problems & Pests

Root rot or other fungal problems may occur. Slugs may be attracted to the young foliage.

Summer Forget-Me-Not

Cape Forget-Me-Not

Anchusa

Height: 9–24" **Spread:** about 12" **Flower color:** blue, pink, white

LOVERS OF BLUE WILL BE QUICKLY SMITTEN BY THIS EASY-CARE annual. It features delicate, true blue flowers that cover the plants from June through August. This is a great annual for the front of the border, whether grown in small patches repeated along the garden edge or massed in larger gardens. All are sensational in flower boxes, with 'Blue Angel' being the most commonly grown for this purpose.

This plant originated in South Africa in the area of the Cape of Good Hope, which is where the name cape forget-me-not was derived.

Planting

Seeding: Indoors in early winter; direct sow in fall

Planting out: After last frost

Spacing: 8–12"

Growing

This plant grows best in a location that gets **full sun** but is not too hot. The soil should be **poor** or **average** and **well drained.** Starting seeds indoors in early winter will encourage more flowers. Seed is sown in fall to have flowers the following year. Chill seeds one week before planting.

Tips

Use summer forget-me-not as a border filler. The larger varieties are most attractive mixed with other plants in a border. The smaller varieties can be mass planted together to create a sea of blue in a border. Dwarf varieties may need to be planted closer together than other varieties of summer forget-me-not.

Trimming the plants back as they finish blooming will encourage them to keep on flowering throughout summer.

A. capensis cultivar

Recommended

A. capensis is an erect biennial grown as an annual. It grows 18–24" tall and about 12" wide, bearing abundant, white-centered, deep blue to pink flowers in late spring and summer. **'Blue Angel'** has intense blue flowers. These compact plants grow 9–12" tall. **'Blue Heaven'** grows 18–24" tall and produces masses of abundant, blue flowers. **'Dawn'** has blue, pink or white flowers. The plants grow 18–24" tall.

Problems & Pests

Summer forget-me-not has occasional problems with cutworms and vine weevil larvae.

A. capensis with calendula and petunia

Sunflower

Helianthus

Height: dwarf varieties 24–36"; giants up to 10' **Spread:** 12–24"
Flower color: most commonly yellow but also orange, red, brown, cream, bicolored; typically with brown, black, purple or rusty red centers

THE GREAT GARDEN WRITER HENRY MITCHELL WROTE, 'THE sunflower is an American flower, of course. It would do quite well, as far as I am concerned, as the national flower, and while we think of it, when we think of Kansas and similar outposts of the empire, it flourishes virtually everywhere, provided it receives sun and heat.' He is correct, of course. It's impossible not to love a flower with the inimitable fearlessness of the sunflower, no matter how brazen its appearance. Grow sunflowers for the eye-catching, defiant joy they express.

Plant a row of sunflowers at the back of the vegetable garden, or use one of the lower varieties against a split-rail fence.

Planting

Seeding: Indoors in late winter; direct sow in spring

Planting out: After last frost

Spacing: 12–24"

Growing

Sunflower grows best in **full sun.** The soil should be of **average fertility, humus rich, moist** and **well drained.**

The annual sunflower is an excellent plant for children to grow. The seeds are big and easy to handle, and they germinate quickly. The plants grow steadily upwards, and their progress can be measured until the flower finally appears on top of the tall plant. If planted along the wall of a two-story house, beneath an upstairs window, the progress can be observed from above as well as below, and the flowers will be easier to see.

H. annuus cultivars (photos this page)

Tips

Use the lower-growing sunflower varieties in beds and borders. The tall varieties are effective at the backs of borders and make good screens and temporary hedges. The tallest varieties may need staking.

H. annuus is grown as a crop for its seeds, which are used for roasting, snacking, baking or producing oil or flour.

Birds will flock to the ripening seedheads of your sunflowers, quickly plucking out the tightly packed seeds. If you plan to keep the seeds to eat, you may need to place a mesh net, the sort used to keep birds out of cherry trees, around the flowerheads until the seeds ripen. The net can be a bit of a nuisance and does not look very nice, so most gardeners leave the flowers to the birds and buy seeds for eating.

Recommended

H. annuus (common sunflower) is often considered weedy, but the development of many new cultivars has revived the use of this plant. **'Music Box'** is a branching plant that grows about 30" tall and has flowers in all colors, including some bicolors. **'Prado Red'** bears deep mahogany flowers and grows up to 5'. **'Ring of Fire'** has red flower petals with bright gold tips and large, black centers. **'Russian Giant'** grows up to 10' tall and bears yellow flowers that develop large seeds. **'Soyara'** has bright orange flowers on well-branched plants. **'Teddy Bear'** has rather fuzzy-looking double flowers on compact plants 24–36" tall. **'Valentine'** bears creamy yellow flowers and grows up to 5'. **'Velvet Queen'** is a branching cultivar that bears many crimson red flowers.

Problems & Pests

Powdery mildew may affect these plants.

Leave the plants in the garden over the winter for a natural bird feeder.

'Teddy Bear' (below)

Swan River Daisy

Brachyscome (Brachycome)

Height: 6–18" **Spread:** equal to or slightly greater than height
Flower color: blue, pink, white, purple; usually with yellow centers

SWAN RIVER DAISIES ARE A CHEERFUL AND TROUBLE-FREE addition to the northern garden, well suited to the front of the border. Slender stems rise from appealing, fern-like foliage bearing great numbers of sweetly scented, daisy-like flowers throughout the growing season. All varieties are exceptional for use in containers, flower boxes and hanging baskets though containers must be placed in sheltered spots that allow for a break from intense afternoon sun.

This Australian plant takes its name from the Swan, a river of southwestern Australia.

Planting

Seeding: Indoors in late winter; direct sow in mid-spring

Planting out: Early spring

Spacing: 12"

Growing

Swan River daisy prefers **full sun** but benefits from light shade in the afternoon. The soil should be **fertile** and **well drained**. Allow the soil to dry between waterings.

Plant out early because cool spring weather encourages compact, sturdy growth. This plant is frost tolerant and tends to die back when summer gets too hot. Cut it back if it begins to fade, and don't plant it in hot areas of the garden.

Tips

This versatile plant edges beds nicely and works well in rock gardens, mixed containers, hanging baskets and fresh arrangements.

Combine Swan River daisy with plants that mature later in the season. As Swan River daisy fades in July, its companions will be filling in and beginning to flower.

Recommended

B. **hybrids** are all heat-tolerant selections. **'Compact Pink'** grows 9–12" tall with dense, lacy foliage and light pink flowers. **'Hot Candy'** grows 6–10" tall and has larger leaves than other Swan River daisies. The flowers are bright pink. **'Toucan Tango'** grows 6–12" tall, with an equal spread. Bright lavender to violet blue flowers bloom from late spring to fall.

B. iberidifolia forms a bushy, spreading, 18" mound of feathery foliage. Blue-purple or pink-purple, daisy-like flowers are borne all summer. **Bravo Series** plants grow 8–10" tall, bearing flowers in white, blue, purple or pink, which bloom profusely in a cool but bright spot in the garden. Plants in the **Splendor Series** grow 9–12" tall and have dark-centered flowers in pink, purple or white.

Problems & Pests

Aphids, slugs and snails cause occasional trouble for this plant.

B. iberidifolia

Sweet Alyssum

Alyssum

Lobularia

Height: 3–12" **Spread:** 6–24" **Flower color:** pink, purple, peach, white, bicolored

SWEET ALYSSUM IS ONE OF THE MOST POPULAR and useful edging plants available to northern gardeners, and for many years has been a mainstay of the front of the garden bed. Alyssums look fabulous planted right next to stone edging in raised beds, where their sprawling mounds of tiny flowers cascade over and between the stones. Though they do not tolerate foot traffic, they are suitable for planting in the cracks between patio stones just off the traffic path. Use them along the edge of containers as well, for they thrive in sun and heat.

Planting

Seeding: Indoors in late winter; direct sow in spring

Planting out: Once soil has warmed

Spacing: 8–10"

Growing

Sweet alyssum prefers **full sun** but tolerates light shade. **Well-drained** soil of **average fertility** is preferred, but poor soil is tolerated. This plant dislikes having its roots disturbed, so if starting it indoors, use peat pots or pellets. Trim sweet alyssum back occasionally over the summer to keep it flowering and looking good.

Leave sweet alyssum plants out all winter. In spring, remove the previous year's growth to expose self-sowed seedlings below.

Tips

Sweet alyssum will creep around rock gardens, on rock walls and along the edges of beds. It is an excellent choice for seeding into cracks and crevices of walkway and patio stones, and once established, it readily reseeds. It is also good for filling in spaces between taller plants in borders and in mixed containers.

Recommended

L. maritima forms a low, spreading mound of foliage. The entire plant appears to be covered in tiny blossoms when it is in full flower. **'Pastel Carpet'** bears flowers in rose, white, violet and mauve. **'Snow Crystal'** bears large, bright white flowers profusely all summer. **Wonderland Series** plants offer a mix of all colors on compact plants.

Problems & Pests

Sweet alyssum rarely has problems but is sometimes afflicted with downy mildew.

Alyssum, *the original genus name for this annual, comes from the Greek and means 'not madness,' referring to the belief that the plant could cure rabies.*

L. maritima cultivar

Sweet Pea

Lathyrus

Height: 12"–6' **Spread:** 6–18" **Flower color:** pink, red, purple, blue, salmon, pale yellow, peach, white, bicolored

THE DELICATE FLOWERS OF THIS OLD-FASHIONED FAVORITE FLOAT like butterflies throughout the pleasant foliage, making sweet pea one of America's favorite climbing plants. Sweet peas flourish in cool weather, making them an excellent choice for northern gardens. Climbers listed on the next page need little more than a pole to begin their ascent and will even scale a dry-stack stone wall. The Supersnoop Series was developed to allow gardeners the fun of growing the plant as a non-climbing addition to the garden bed, and they're wonderful when grown as the only plant in mid-sized containers.

Sweet pea blossoms make attractive, long-lasting cut flowers. Cutting the flowers encourages still more blooms.

Planting

Seeding: Direct sow in early spring

Spacing: 6–12"

Growing

Sweet pea prefers **full sun** but tolerates light shade. The soil should be **fertile,** high in **organic matter, moist** and **well drained.** Fertilize very lightly with a low-nitrogen fertilizer during the flowering season. This plant will tolerate light frost. Deadhead all spent blooms.

Soak seeds in water for 24 hours or nick them with a nail file before planting them. Planting a second crop of sweet peas about a month after the first one will ensure a longer blooming period.

Tips

Sweet pea will grow up poles, trellises and fences or over rocks. The low-growing varieties form low, shrubby mounds.

To help prevent diseases from afflicting your sweet pea plants, avoid planting in the same location two years in a row.

Recommended

L. odoratus is the parent of many cultivars. **Bijou Series** plants are popular heat-resistant varieties that grow 18" tall, with an equal spread. It needs no support structure to grow on. **'Bouquet Mix'** is a tall, climbing variety. **'Cupid'** is a dwarf cultivar with fragrant, light pink and white bicolored flowers. **'Painted Lady'** has very fragrant flowers that are deep pink and white bicolored. **Supersnoop Series** plants are sturdy bush types that need no support. The flowers are fragrant. Pinch the tips of the long stems to encourage low growth.

L. odoratus cultivar

Problems & Pests

Slugs and snails may eat the foliage of young plants. Root rot, mildew, rust and leaf spot may also afflict sweet pea occasionally.

L. odoratus cultivar with Stoke's aster

Transvaal Daisy

Gerbera Daisy

Gerbera

Height: 8–24" **Spread:** up to 24" **Flower color:** pink, red, orange, yellow

THOUGH I AM HESITANT TO CRITICIZE ANY FLOWER THAT HAS leapt so quickly to the forefront of northern nursery sales as the Transvaal daisy, these plants are boldly different in form and flower from most annuals and perennials grown in the region, so you'll either love their uniqueness or be wary of their somewhat artificial look. A few planted here and there tend to look like plastic intruders, and their large leaves resemble Boston lettuce, not the plant's best feature. If you love the look—there's no denying that the blooms are large and colorful—use them in containers. They also mix well with true tropicals in an eclectic-style garden.

Transvaal daisy is also popular as a short-lived houseplant.

Planting

Seeding: Not recommended; basal cuttings can be taken in summer

Planting out: Late spring

Spacing: 14–18"

Growing

Transvaal daisy prefers **full sun** but tolerates partial shade. The soil should be **well drained,** have plenty of **organic matter** worked in and be of **average to high fertility**. To keep the crown of the plant dry, set the crown just above the soil line. If your soil is poorly drained, use a raised bed. Allow soil to almost dry out between waterings.

Transvaal daisy can be quite difficult to grow from seed. It is easier to purchase plants in spring. If you like a challenge and want to attempt to grow the plants from seed, use only very fresh seed, because the seeds

lose viability very quickly. When seeding indoors, start them in December or January and cover the seed flat or pot with clear plastic to maintain high humidity while the seeds are germinating. When transplanting, be careful not to plant too deeply.

Tips

Transvaal daisies prefer warm weather. In the garden they make an impressive addition to annual beds, borders and mixed containers.

Transvaal daisy is popular as a cut flower. For longer-lasting flowers, slit the bottoms of the stems up one inch to help them absorb water. Do this cut under warm water for maximum water saturation in the stem.

Recommended

G. jamesonii is a clump-forming plant 12–18" tall and 24" wide. Yellow-centered flowers in solid shades of yellow, orange, apricot and red bloom from late spring to late summer. **'California Giants'** grow to 24" tall, with flowers in red, orange, yellow and pink. **'Happipot'** has compact plants that grow to 8" tall, with mixed flower colors. **'Skipper'** has smaller leaves and shorter stems and grows 8–10" tall. It is good for edging beds or for containers.

Problems & Pests

Slugs and snails, crown rot and root rot are the most common problems. Leaf miners, aphids, thrips and whiteflies can also be troublesome.

Verbena

Garden Verbena

Verbena

Height: 4"–5' **Spread:** 10–36" **Flower color:** red, pink, purple, blue, yellow, scarlet, salmon, peach, white; usually with white centers

THE MANY CULTIVARS OF VERBENA ARE EXCEPTIONAL PLANTS FOR containers in the north, where their colorful, mounding clusters of small flowers, many with a white eye, are the perfect foil for more erect, larger-flowered annuals. Plant hybridizers have spent much time developing new varieties, a wide range of which will be available as transplants at your local nursery. In containers or the garden bed, experiment with combinations of verbena and any taller, vertical flower, such as salvia, African daisy and pot marigold. The plant also provides season-long color when popped in here and there between perennials.

If your plants become leggy or overgrown, cut them back by one-half to tidy them and promote lots of fall blooms.

Planting

Seeding: Indoors in mid-winter

Planting out: After last frost

Spacing: 10–36"

Growing

Verbenas grow best in **full sun**. The soil should be **fertile** and very **well drained**. Pinch back young plants for bushy growth.

Chill seeds one week before sowing. Moisten the soil before sowing seeds. Do not cover the seeds with soil. Place the entire seed tray or pot in darkness, and water only if the soil becomes very dry. Once the seeds germinate, move them into the light.

Tips

Use verbenas on rock walls and in beds, borders, rock gardens, containers, hanging baskets and window boxes. They make good substitutes for ivy-leaved geraniums where the sun is hot and where a roof overhang keeps the mildew-prone verbenas dry.

V. x *hybrida* mixed hybrids

The Romans, it is said, believed verbena could rekindle the flames of dying love. They named it Herba Veneris, *'plant of Venus.'*

V. canadensis

V. bonariensis below petunias

'Homestead Purple' was a chance discovery by horticulturalists Allan Armitage and Michael Dirr on a Georgia homestead.

Recommended

V. bonariensis forms a low clump of foliage from which tall, stiff, flower-bearing stems emerge. The small, purple flowers are held in clusters. This plant grows up to 5' tall but spreads only 18–24". It may survive a mild winter, and it will self-seed. Butterflies love this plant.

V. canadensis (clump verbena, rose vervain) is a low-growing, spreading plant native to south-central and southeastern North America. It grows up to 18" tall and up to 36" wide. Clusters of pink flowers appear from mid-summer to fall. It may survive a mild winter. Plants in the **Babylon Series** grow to 7" tall, resist mildew and flower early. This series produces abundant flowers in shades of pink, purple and red. **'Homestead Purple'** is the most common cultivar; it is more common than the species in gardens. It bears dark purple flowers all summer and resists

V. x *hybrida* Tapien Series

mildew. **Tukana Series** plants also grow to 7" tall and produce flowers in shades of blue, salmon, scarlet and white.

V. x *hybrida* is a bushy plant that may be upright or spreading. It bears clusters of small flowers in shades of white, purple, blue, pink, red or yellow. **Aztec Series** from Simply Beautiful includes plants 16–18" tall and 10–12" wide. They feature flowers in an impressive array of purples, pinks, reds and white. **'Imagination'** (*V.* x *speciosa* **'Imagination'**) grows 12–24" tall and 24–36" wide. This All-America Selections winner produces clusters of intense violet blue flowers. **'Peaches and Cream'** is a spreading plant with flowers that open a soft peach color and fade to white. **Romance Series** plants grow up to 8–10" tall and have red, pink, purple or white flowers with white eyes. **'Showtime'** bears brightly colored flowers on compact plants that grow up to 10" tall and spread 18". **Tapien Series** plants from Proven Winners grow 4–6" tall and 10–18" wide. These low-growing, well-branched plants flower in white and shades of pink and purple. **Temari Series** plants resist mildew, tolerate heat and have vigorous, spreading growth. The flowers come in a range of colors on plants 8–14" tall.

V. pendula **Superbena Series** from Proven Winners includes vigorous, upright to trailing plants 6–12" tall and 10–14" wide. The plants have excellent mildew resistance and boast large flowers in intense shades of red, pink and purple.

Problems & Pests

Aphids, whiteflies, slugs and snails may be troublesome. Avoid fungal problems by making sure there is good air circulation around verbena plants.

V. x *hybrida* cultivars

Violet
Pansy, Johnny-Jump-Up
Viola

Height: 3–10" **Spread:** 4–16" **Flower color:** blue, purple, red, orange, yellow, pink, white, multi-colored

UNDERTAKE A REGIMEN OF REGULAR DEADHEADING OF YOUR violets, and they will bloom longer than most other plants in northern gardens. Every year, it seems, there are wonderful new flower colors and color combinations from which to choose. Violets will handle late spring frosts and are wonderful in mass plantings and as edgings, yet they are just as desirable in containers. Like most annuals, you should plant them closer than most plant tags suggest, 6" at the most, so that their attractive, lobed foliage and relatively large blooms quickly form a thick carpet of color and texture.

These versatile plants are perfect for planting early in the season when frost still threatens.

Planting

Seeding: Indoors in early winter or mid-summer

Planting out: Early spring or early fall

Spacing: 6"

Growing

Violets prefer **full sun** but tolerate partial shade. The soil should be **fertile, moist** and **well drained**.

Violets do best when the weather is cool. They may die back completely in summer. Plants may rejuvenate in fall, but it is often easier to plant new ones in fall and not take up summer garden space with annuals that don't look their best.

Direct sowing is not recommended. Sow seeds indoors in early winter for spring flowers and in mid-summer for fall and early winter blooms. More seeds will germinate if they are kept in darkness until they sprout. Place seed trays in a dark closet or cover with dark plastic or layers of newspaper to block out the light.

Tips

Violets can be used in beds and borders, and they are popular for mixing in with spring-flowering bulbs. They can also be grown in containers. The large-flowered pansies are preferable for early-spring color among primroses in garden beds.

Recommended

V. cornuta (horned violet, viola) is low-growing, about 6" tall and 12–16" wide. The flowers are smaller than those of pansies and larger than Johnny-jump-ups, usually in shades

Perfume bottles with narrow necks make wonderful small vases for displaying the cut flowers of violets. The more you pick, the more profusely the plants will bloom. These flowers are also among the easiest to press between sheets of wax paper, weighted down with stacks of books.

V. x *wittrockiana* with tulips

V. x wittrockiana

of blue, purple or white with the distinctive and charming 'face' pattern violets are known for. **'Bambini'** produces flowers in a wider range of colors, including shades of pink, yellow, orange, blue, purple and white. The popular **Sorbet Series** plants have a wide color range and tolerate cold. Planted in fall, they will flower until the ground freezes and may surprise you with another show in spring. 'Sorbet Yesterday, Today & Tomorrow' bears flowers that open white and gradually turn purple as they mature.

V. tricolor (Johnny-jump-up) is a popular species. It grows 3–6" tall and 4–6" wide. The flowers are purple, white and yellow, usually in combination, although several varieties have flowers in a single color, frequently purple. This plant thrives in gravel. **'Bowles Black'** has dark purple flowers that appear almost black. The center of each flower is yellow. **'Helen Mound'** ('Helen

V. x w. 'Ultima Morpho'

Mount') bears large flowers in the traditional, cheerful purple, yellow and white combination.

V. x ***wittrockiana*** (pansy) plants grow 8–10" tall and 6–12" wide. The flowers come in blue, purple, red, orange, yellow, pink or white, often multi-colored or with face-like markings. **'Floral Dance'** is popular for spring and fall displays because it is quite cold hardy; it has flowers in a variety of solid colors and multi-colors. **Imperial Series** plants bear large flowers in a range of unique colors. For example, 'Imperial Frosty Rose' has flowers with deep rose pink centers that gradually pale to white near the edges of the petals. **Joker Series** plants have bicolored or multi-colored flowers with distinctive face-like markings. The flowers come in all colors. **'Maxim Marina'** bears light blue flowers with white-rimmed, dark blue blotches at the center. This cultivar tolerates both high and low temperatures. **'Ultima Morpho'** is a unique bicolor. Among its variations are azure to mid-blue upper petals over bright lemon yellow lower petals. It is a 2002 All-America Selections winner. The **Watercolor Series** is a newer group of cultivars with flowers in delicate pastel shades.

Violet flowers are edible and make delightful garnishes on salads and desserts. Make candied violets by brushing the flowers with whipped egg white and sprinkling them with superfine sugar. Allow them to dry overnight.

Problems & Pests

Slugs and snails can be problems. Fungal diseases can be avoided through good air circulation and good drainage.

V. tricolor

Wishbone Flower

Torenia

Height: 6–12" **Spread:** 6–12" **Flower color:** purple, pink, blue, white; often bicolored with a yellow spot on the lower petal

I DISCOVERED WISHBONE FLOWER FAR TOO LATE IN MY gardening experience, and I wish I had known about these charming, shade-loving plants far earlier. Plants in the Summer Wave Series are the salvation of my fairly shaded, west-facing flower boxes. They mound up then trail over the sides, covering the boxes with bicolored, trumpet-shaped blooms from late June to frost. Wishbone flower does not do well in dense or dappled shade areas where it receives no direct sunlight; find a spot with two to three hours of direct sun at any time of day, and this plant should flourish. It is widely available in spring as a transplant.

Planting

Seeding: Indoors in late winter

Planting out: After last-frost date

Spacing: 6–8"

Growing

Wishbone flower prefers **light shade** but tolerates partial and full shade. The soil should be **fertile, light, humus rich** and **moist**. This plant requires regular watering.

Don't cover the seeds when planting; they need light to germinate.

Tips

Wishbone flower can be massed in a shaded bed or border, used as an edging plant or added to a mixed container or hanging basket. It makes a nice change in shade gardens if you find yourself overusing impatiens. Try wishbone flower near a water feature, where the soil may remain moist for extended periods.

Recommended

T. fournieri is a bushy, rounded to upright plant. It grows up to 12" tall, with an equal or lesser spread. Its purple flowers have yellow throats. **Clown Series** plants are compact, growing 6–10" tall. The flowers may be purple, blue, pink or white. **Duchess Series** plants are also compact, growing only up to 6" tall, but they bear larger flowers in a range of colors. Plants in the **Summer Wave Series** are fast-growing and heat-loving. The series includes 'Amethyst,' with rich magenta purple flowers; 'Blue,' with violet-tinged blue flowers; and 'Large Violet,' with large, deep violet flowers.

Wishbone flower is one of the few annuals that tolerates constantly damp (but not waterlogged) soils.

T. fournieri cultivar

Problems & Pests

Fungal problems can occur in overly wet soils. Moist but not soggy soils are ideal.

T. fournieri

Zinnia

Zinnia

Height: 6–36" **Spread:** 12" **Flower color:** red, yellow, gold, green, purple, orange, pink, white, maroon, brown

HOW I HATE IT WHEN A FLOWER I DON'T FANCY BECOMES ONE I adore. That's my experience with zinnias, but in my defense I must say that the gangly, drunken, mildewy variety I grew—once—20 years ago couldn't be found in the trade now if lives depended on it. Experiment with the new varieties of *Z. haageana* and the *Z.* Profusion Series, which lead away from the older, cushion form of *Z. elegans.* Zinnias have a wide range of uses in both formal and informal gardens, in containers and as cut flowers.

Planting

Seeding: Indoors in late winter; direct sow after last frost

Planting out: After last frost

Spacing: 6–12"

Growing

Zinnias grow best in **full sun**. The soil should be **fertile**, rich in **organic matter, moist** and **well drained.** When starting seeds indoors, plant them in individual peat pots to avoid disturbing the roots when transplanting.

Deadhead zinnias to keep them flowering and looking their best. To keep mildew from the leaves, plant mildew-resistant varieties and avoid wetting the foliage when you water.

Tips

Zinnias are useful in beds, borders, containers and cutting gardens. The dwarf varieties can be used as edging

'Profusion White'

Z. e. 'California Giants'

plants. These plants often bloom right up to the first frost and are wonderful for fall color. Combine the rounded zinnia flowers with the spiky blooms of sun-loving salvia, or use the taller varieties in front of sunflowers.

Recommended

Z. elegans and its cultivars bear flowers in several forms, including

Z. haageana cultivar

single, double and cactus flowered. On a cactus-flowered bloom, the petals appear to be rolled into tubes like the spines of a cactus. **'California Giants'** are bushy plants that grow to 36" and bear large, double flowers in a wide range of colors. **'Dreamland'** bears up to 4" wide double flowers on compact plants that reach a height of about 10". **'Peter Pan'** grows up to 12" tall, but it starts blooming early at 6", with flowers in mixed colors. **Thumbelina**

Though zinnias are quite drought tolerant, they will grow best if watered thoroughly when the soil dries out. Use a soaker hose to avoid wetting the leaves. The name zinnia honors Johann Gottfried Zinn (1727–59), the German botany professor who first grew one of the South American zinnias from seed.

Z. e. 'California Giants'

Series plants have small flowers in all colors on dwarf, 6", weather-resistant plants.

Z. haageana (*Z. angustifolia;* Mexican zinnia) is a bushy plant with narrow leaves. It grows 6–24" tall, spreads 12" and bears bright orange, daisy-like flowers. This species tolerates heat and drought and resists pests. **'Crystal White'** bears white, daisy-like flowers on plants that grow 6–8" tall. It makes a wonderful edger for beds and borders. **'Persian Carpet'** bears bicolored and tricolored flowers in orange, red, yellow, gold, maroon and brown.

Z. **Profusion Series** are fast-growing, mildew-resistant, compact hybrids. These All-America Selections grow 10–18" tall and bear flowers in bright cherry red, orange or white.

Z. e. 'Dreamland Yellow'

Problems & Pests

Zinnias can be prone to mildew and other fungal problems. Prevent such problems by ensuring good air circulation and drainage for the plants and by planting resistant varieties.

Z. elegans cultivars

Quick Reference Chart

HEIGHT LEGEND: Low: < 12" • Medium: 12–24" • Tall: > 24"

SPECIES	COLOR									SOWING		HEIGHT		
	White	Pink	Red	Orange	Yellow	Blue	Purple	Green	Foliage	Indoors	Direct	Low	Medium	Tall
Ageratum	•	•	•			•	•			•	•	•	•	•
Amaranth			•		•			•	•	•	•			•
Angel's Trumpet	•	•			•		•			•			•	•
Annual Chrysanthemum	•		•		•		•			•	•		•	•
Annual Phlox	•	•	•		•	•	•				•	•	•	
Baby Blue-Eyes	•					•	•				•	•		
Baby's Breath	•	•					•			•	•		•	•
Bachelor's Buttons	•	•	•			•	•			•	•		•	•
Begonia	•	•	•	•	•				•	•		•	•	
Black-eyed Susan			•	•	•					•	•	•	•	•
Black-eyed Susan Vine	•			•	•		•			•	•			•
Browallia	•					•	•			•		•	•	
Calendula				•	•					•	•	•	•	
California Poppy		•	•	•	•						•	•	•	
Candytuft	•	•	•				•			•	•	•		
Canterbury Bells	•	•				•	•			•			•	•
Cape Marigold	•	•	•	•	•					•	•		•	
Celosia		•	•	•	•		•			•	•	•	•	•
China Aster	•	•	•		•	•	•			•	•	•	•	•
Cleome	•	•					•			•	•	•	•	•
Coleus							•		•	•	•	•	•	•
Coreopsis			•	•	•					•	•		•	•
Cosmos	•	•	•	•	•		•			•	•		•	•
Cup Flower	•					•	•			•		•		
Dahlberg Daisy				•	•					•	•	•		
Dahlia	•	•	•	•	•		•			•	•		•	•
Dianthus	•	•	•				•			•	•	•	•	•
Diascia	•	•	•	•	•					•		•	•	

Quick Reference Chart

HARDINESS			LIGHT				SOIL CONDITIONS							SPECIES
Hardy	Half-hardy	Tender	Sun	Part Shade	Light Shade	Shade	Moist	Well Drained	Dry	Fertile	Average	Poor	Page Number	
		•	•	•			•	•		•			48	Ageratum
		•	•					•			•	•	52	Amaranth
		•	•				•	•		•			56	Angel's Trumpet
•	•		•	•				•			•		60	Annual Chrysanthemum
•			•	•			•	•		•			62	Annual Phlox
•			•	•			•	•		•			64	Baby Blue-Eyes
•			•					•	•			•	66	Baby's Breath
•			•	•			•	•	•	•			68	Bachelor's Buttons
		•	•	•	•			•		•			70	Begonia
	•		•	•			•	•	•		•		76	Black-Eyed Susan
		•	•	•	•		•	•		•			80	Black-Eyed Susan Vine
		•	•	•	•	•		•		•			82	Browallia
•			•	•				•			•		84	Calendula
•			•					•	•		•	•	86	California Poppy
•			•	•				•			•	•	88	Candytuft
•			•	•			•	•		•			90	Canterbury Bells
		•	•					•	•	•			92	Cape Marigold
		•	•					•		•			94	Celosia
			•	•			•	•		•			98	China Aster
	•		•	•			•	•	•	•	•	•	100	Cleome
		•	•	•	•	•	•	•		•	•		104	Coleus
•			•					•	•	•	•		108	Coreopsis
		•	•					•	•		•	•	110	Cosmos
	•		•	•			•	•			•		114	Cup Flower
•			•					•			•	•	116	Dahlberg Daisy
		•	•				•	•			•		118	Dahlia
•			•	•	•			•			•		122	Dianthus
	•		•				•	•		•			126	Diascia

Quick Reference Chart

HEIGHT LEGEND: Low: < 12" • Medium: 12–24" • Tall: > 24"

SPECIES	COLOR									SOWING		HEIGHT		
	White	Pink	Red	Orange	Yellow	Blue	Purple	Green	Foliage	Indoors	Direct	Low	Medium	Tall
Dusty Miller	•				•				•	•			•	
Dwarf Morning Glory		•				•	•			•	•	•	•	
English Daisy	•	•	•							•		•		
Felicia						•				•	•	•	•	
Flowering Flax	•	•	•			•	•				•		•	•
Flowering Tobacco	•	•	•				•	•		•	•	•	•	•
Forget-Me-Not	•	•				•				•	•	•		
Four-O'Clocks	•	•	•	•	•		•			•	•	•	•	
Fuchsia	•	•	•	•			•					•	•	•
Gaura	•	•								•				•
Gazania	•	•	•	•	•					•	•	•	•	
Geranium	•	•	•	•			•			•		•	•	•
Globe Amaranth	•	•	•	•			•			•		•	•	•
Godetia	•	•	•				•				•	•		•
Heliotrope	•					•	•			•		•	•	•
Hollyhock	•	•	•	•	•		•			•				•
Impatiens	•	•	•	•	•		•			•		•	•	•
Lantana	•	•	•	•	•		•					•	•	•
Larkspur	•	•				•	•			•	•		•	•
Lavatera	•	•	•				•			•	•		•	•
Lisianthus	•	•			•	•	•			•		•	•	•
Lobelia	•	•				•	•			•		•		
Love-in-a-Mist	•	•				•	•			•	•		•	
Madagascar Periwinkle	•	•	•							•		•	•	
Marigold			•	•	•					•		•	•	•
Mexican Sunflower				•	•					•	•			•
Monkey Flower		•	•	•	•					•		•		
Morning Glory	•	•	•	•	•	•	•			•	•		•	•

Quick Reference Chart

Hardy	Half-hardy	Tender	Sun	Part Shade	Light Shade	Shade	Moist	Well Drained	Dry	Fertile	Average	Poor	Page Number	SPECIES
	HARDINESS			LIGHT				SOIL CONDITIONS						
	•		•	•	•			•			•		130	Dusty Miller
		•	•					•			•	•	132	Dwarf Morning Glory
	•		•	•	•		•			•	•		134	English Daisy
	•		•					•			•		136	Felicia
•			•	•				•	•		•		138	Flowering Flax
		•	•	•	•		•	•		•			140	Flowering Tobacco
•			•	•	•		•	•		•			144	Forget-Me-Not
		•	•	•			•	•	•	•			146	Four O'Clocks
		•		•	•		•	•		•			148	Fuchsia
	•		•	•			•	•		•			152	Gaura
		•	•	•				•	•		•	•	154	Gazania
		•	•	•				•		•			156	Geranium
		•	•					•	•		•		160	Globe Amaranth
•			•	•	•			•	•		•	•	162	Godetia
		•	•				•	•		•			164	Heliotrope
•			•	•				•		•	•		168	Hollyhock
		•	•	•	•	•	•	•		•			170	Impatiens
	•		•	•			•	•	•	•			174	Lantana
•			•		•			•		•			176	Larkspur
•			•	•				•			•		178	Lavatera
	•		•	•	•			•			•		182	Lisianthus
•			•	•			•	•		•			184	Lobelia
•			•					•			•		186	Love-in-a-Mist
		•	•	•			•	•	•				188	Madagascar Periwinkle
	•	•	•					•	•		•		190	Marigold
		•	•					•	•		•	•	194	Mexican Sunflower
	•	•		•	•		•			•			196	Monkey Flower
		•	•					•			•	•	198	Morning Glory

Quick Reference Chart

HEIGHT LEGEND: Low: < 12" • Medium: 12–24" • Tall: > 24"

SPECIES	COLOR									SOWING		HEIGHT		
	White	Pink	Red	Orange	Yellow	Blue	Purple	Green	Foliage	Indoors	Direct	Low	Medium	Tall
Musk Mallow	•	•	•	•	•					•	•		•	•
Nasturtium		•	•	•	•					•	•	•	•	•
Nemesia	•	•	•	•	•	•	•			•		•	•	
Ornamental Kale									•	•	•		•	
Osteospermum	•	•	•	•	•		•			•		•	•	
Painted-Tongue			•	•	•	•	•			•	•		•	
Pentas	•	•	•				•			•	•		•	
Petunia	•	•	•			•	•			•		•	•	
Pimpernel	•	•	•			•				•		•	•	
Pincushion Flower	•	•	•			•	•			•	•		•	•
Polka Dot Plant							•		•	•			•	
Poor Man's Orchid	•	•	•	•	•		•			•	•	•	•	
Poppy	•	•	•	•	•		•				•		•	•
Portulaca	•	•	•	•	•		•			•		•		
Salvia	•	•	•	•	•	•	•			•	•		•	•
Snapdragon	•	•	•	•	•		•			•	•	•	•	•
Statice	•	•	•	•	•	•	•			•	•		•	
Stock	•	•	•		•		•			•	•	•	•	•
Summer Forget-Me-Not	•	•				•				•	•	•	•	
Sunflower			•	•	•					•	•			•
Swan River Daisy	•	•				•	•			•	•	•	•	
Sweet Alyssum	•	•					•			•	•	•		
Sweet Pea	•	•	•	•	•	•	•				•		•	•
Transvaal Daisy		•	•	•	•							•	•	
Verbena	•	•	•	•	•	•	•			•		•	•	•
Violet	•	•	•	•	•	•	•			•		•		
Wishbone Flower	•	•				•	•			•		•		
Zinnia	•	•	•	•	•		•	•		•	•	•	•	•

Quick Reference Chart

HARDINESS			LIGHT				SOIL CONDITIONS							SPECIES
Hardy	Half-hardy	Tender	Sun	Part Shade	Light Shade	Shade	Moist	Well Drained	Dry	Fertile	Average	Poor	Page Number	
		•	•					•		•			202	Musk Mallow
		•	•	•			•	•	•		•	•	204	Nasturtium
		•	•				•	•		•	•		208	Nemesia
•			•	•			•	•		•			210	Ornamental Kale
		•	•				•	•			•		212	Osteospermum
		•	•					•		•			216	Painted-Tongue
	•		•				•	•		•			218	Pentas
	•		•					•		•	•		220	Petunia
		•	•				•	•		•			224	Pimpernel
	•		•					•		•	•		226	Pincushion Flower
		•	•	•	•		•	•			•		228	Polka Dot Plant
		•	•	•			•	•		•			230	Poor Man's Orchid
•			•					•		•			234	Poppy
		•	•					•	•			•	238	Portulaca
	•	•	•	•	•		•	•		•	•		240	Salvia
	•		•	•	•			•		•			244	Snapdragon
		•	•					•	•		•	•	248	Statice
•			•	•			•	•			•		250	Stock
		•	•					•			•	•	252	Summer Forget-Me-Not
•			•				•	•			•		254	Sunflower
	•		•	•	•			•		•			258	Swan River Daisy
•			•	•	•			•			•		260	Sweet Alyssum
•			•	•	•		•	•		•			262	Sweet Pea
		•	•	•				•		•	•		264	Transvaal Daisy
•		•	•					•		•			268	Verbena
•			•	•			•	•		•			272	Violet
		•		•	•	•	•			•			276	Wishbone Flower
		•	•				•	•		•			278	Zinnia

Glossary

acid soil: soil with a pH lower than 7.0

alkaline soil: soil with a pH higher than 7.0

annual: a plant that germinates, flowers, sets seed and dies in one growing season

basal leaves: leaves that form from the crown, at the base of the plant

biennial: a plant that germinates and produces stems, roots and leaves in the first growing season; it flowers, sets seed and dies in the second growing season

crown: the part of a plant at or just below soil level where the shoots join the roots

cultivar: a cultivated plant variety with one or more distinct differences from the species, e.g., in flower color, leaf variegation or disease resistance

damping off: fungal disease causing seedlings to rot at soil level and topple over

deadhead: to remove spent flowers to maintain a neat appearance and encourage a longer blooming period

desiccation: drying out of plant tissue, especially foliage

direct sow: to sow seeds directly in the garden soil where the plants are to grow, as opposed to sowing first in pots or flats and transplanting

disbud: to remove some flowerbuds to improve the size or quality of the remaining ones

dormancy: a period of plant inactivity, usually during winter or unfavorable climatic conditions

double flower: a flower with an unusually large number of petals, often caused by mutation of the stamens into petals

forma (f.): a naturally occurring variant of a species; below the level of subspecies in biological classification and similar to variety

genus: a category of biological classification between the species and family levels; the first word in a scientific name indicates the genus

half-hardy: a plant capable of surviving the climatic conditions of a given region if protected from heavy frost or cold

harden off: to gradually acclimatize plants that have been growing in a protective environment (usually indoors) to a more harsh environment (usually outdoors in spring)

hardy: capable of surviving unfavorable conditions, such as cold weather or frost, without protection

humus: decomposed or decomposing organic material in the soil

hybrid: a plant resulting from natural or human-induced cross-breeding between varieties, species or genera; the hybrid expresses features of each parent plant

neutral soil: soil with a pH of 7.0

node: the area on a stem from which a leaf or new shoot grows

pH: a measure of acidity or alkalinity (the lower the pH, the higher the acidity); the pH of soil influences availability of nutrients for plants

perennial: a plant that takes three or more years to complete its life cycle; a herbaceous perennial normally dies back to the ground over winter

potager: a garden that combines function with beauty, often by growing vegetables, herbs and ornamental flowers together in a formal pattern of raised beds

quilled: the narrow, tubular shape of petals or florets of certain flowers

rhizome: a root-like food-storing stem that grows horizontally at or just below soil level, from which new shoots may emerge

rootball: the root mass and surrounding soil of a container-grown plant or a plant dug out of the ground

runner: a modified stem that grows on the soil surface; roots and new shoots are produced at nodes along its length

semi-double flower: a flower with petals that form two or three rings

sepal: segment of the outermost ring of a typical flower; usually green and leaf-like, but may be large, colorful and petal-like

single flower: a flower with a single ring of typically four or five petals

species: the fundamental unit of biological classification, simply defined as a group of interfertile organisms; the original entity from which cultivars and varieties are derived

subshrub: a plant that is somewhat shrubby or woody at the base; tender subshrubs may be grown as annuals

subspecies (subsp.): a naturally occurring, regional form of a species, often isolated from other subspecies but still potentially interfertile with them

taproot: a root system consisting of one long main root with smaller roots branching from it

tender: incapable of surviving the climatic conditions of a given region and requiring protection from frost or cold

tepal: a sepal or petal of a flower, when the petals and sepals are not clearly distinguished from each other

true: the passing of desirable characteristics from the parent plant to seed-grown offspring; also called breeding true to type

tuber: the thick section of a rhizome bearing nodes and buds

variegation: foliage that has more than one color, often patched or striped or bearing differently colored leaf margins

variety (var.): a naturally occurring variant of a species; below the level of subspecies in biological classification

xeriscape: a landscaping method that conserves water by using native and drought-tolerant plants

Pest Control Alternatives

The following organic pest and disease treatments are preferable to harmful chemical products.

Ant Control

Mix 3 c. water, 1 c. white sugar and 4 tsp. liquid boric acid in a pot. Bring just to a boil and remove from heat. Let cool. Pour small amounts of the cooled mix into bottlecaps or other very small containers and place them around the ant-infested area. Also try setting out a mixture of equal parts powdered borax and icing sugar.

Baking Soda & Citrus Oil

Treats both leaf spot and powdery mildew. In a spray bottle, mix 4 tsp. baking soda, 1 tbsp. citrus oil and 1 gal. water. Spray the foliage lightly, including the undersides. Do not pour or spray directly onto soil.

Baking Soda & Horticultural Oil

Confirmed effective against powdery mildew. Mix 4 tsp. baking soda, 1 tbsp. horticultural oil in 1 gal. water. Fill a spray bottle and spray the foliage lightly, including the undersides. Do not pour or spray directly onto soil.

Coffee Grounds Spray

Boil 2 lb. used coffee grounds in 3 gal. water for about 10 minutes. Allow to cool; strain the grounds out. Apply as a spray to control whiteflies.

Compost Tea

Mix 1–2 lb. compost in 5 gal. of water. Let sit for four to seven days. Dilute the mix until it resembles weak tea. Use during normal watering or apply as a foliar spray to prevent or treat fungal diseases.

Fish Emulsion/Seaweed (Kelp)

Usually used as foliar nutrient feeds but also appear to work against fungal diseases either by preventing fungus from spreading to noninfected areas or by changing its growing conditions.

Garlic Spray

Effective to control aphids, leafhoppers, whiteflies, some fungi and nematodes. Soak 6 tbsp. finely minced garlic in 2 tsp. mineral oil for at least 24 hours. Add 1 pt. water and 1½ tsp. liquid dish soap. Stir and strain into a glass container for storage. Combine 1–2 tbsp. of this concentrate with 2 c. water to make a spray. Spray a couple of leaves and check in two days for damage. If no damage, spray the foliage of infested plants thoroughly.

Horticultural Oil

Mix 5 tbsp. horticultural oil per 1 gal. water and apply as a spray for a variety of insect and fungal problems.

Insecticidal Soap

Mix 1 tsp. mild dish detergent, with little to no fragrance or color, or pure soap (biodegradable options are available) with 1 qt. water in a clean spray bottle. Spray the surfaces of insect-infested plants and rinse well within an hour of spraying.

Sulfur and Lime-Sulfur

These products are good preventive measures for fungal diseases. You can purchase ready-made products or wettable powders to mix yourself. Do not spray when the temperature is 90° F or higher or you may damage your plants.

Index of Plant Names

Entries in **bold** type indicate main flower headings.

A

B